THE GUIDE TO MOVING MOM
by
SUSAN PHILLIPS BARI

Published by
Susan Sells New York
New York, NY
A division of The Susan Bari Company

303 E 57th St.
New York, NY 10022
© 2012 Susan Phillips Bari

Other books by Susan Phillips Bari

Breaking Through: Creating Opportunities for Women and Minority Owned Businesses
Partnering for Profit: Success Strategies for Tomorrow's Supply Chain
Yes, I Can Do That!

To sign up for the monthly e-newsletter Susan Sells New York, visit
www.susansellsnewyork.com/newsletter

ISBN: 13: 978-1470063702

Printed in the United States of America
New York, NY

Cheers for Moving Mom

"As millions of Baby Boomers are reaching retirement age, Susan Phillips Bari's Moving Mom is the right book at the right time. It's an honest, thorough and indispensable resource guide for anyone wanting to move a parent (or other loved one) with dignity and grace."

Lindsey Pollak, generational expert and Author of
Getting from College to Career

"Wish I had had this common sense book when my Mom was no longer able to stay in her home. There are so many things to consider, so many decisions to make, and this book allows you to think through things logically to arrive at the right decisions.

—**Mary Cantando,** Author of *The Woman's Advantage*

"Susan brings the same passion exhibited in her long career of helping women and minority businesses to gain traction in the marketplace to Moving Mom. While for entrepreneurs, the work day is never over, we often face another challenge: balancing our personal and business lives with those of a parent facing a major life transition. I know from personal experience and I wish I'd had Susan's sage advice several years ago."   **Susan Solovic,** Author of *It's Your Biz*

"Susan's advice is helpful even if no move is involved. Dealing with aging parents at a distance can be more effectively managed with the tools found in this Guide."

—***Marsha Firestone***, President, Women Presidents' Organization

Dedicated to My Mom

Gertrude Goldberg Phillips
1911-1997

Contents

Acknowledgements

There are many people that have contributed to the development of this book. I must start by thanking my mother, Gertrude Goldberg Phillips. At age 84, my Mom reluctantly gave in to the pleas of her two children to relocate from Boston to Northern Virginia. It took incredible bravery and was an amazing journey for all involved with many unexpected problems and unexpected rewards along the way.

My husband Dick Bari became a best friend and confidant to his mother-in-law and helped ease the transition for her and the burden for me.

I am extremely grateful to the team that has volunteered to donate their expertise to this book. Each of their bios can be found in the appendix to this volume. Ph.D. Lori Sokol reminds us that while we are looking out for the emotional well-being of our parent, we need to watch out for ourselves as well. Barbara Brock brings a keen eye to both the sale of property whether while downsizing or for estate sales and reminds us that staging can help allay transition fears after the move as well as before. Cindy Myer has many years' experience making what to my mind is the most difficult part of the move – the move itself – and provides secrets for making seniors comfortable in their relocation. Attorney Matt Abrams helps us to dot our "i's" and cross those "t's" when making certain that the legal aspects of getting older and of selling property are attended to.

I also want to thank my friends Betty, Lorna and Judy who have contributed their personal stories of dealing with the changes we all must make in altering our living arrangements as we and our families grow older.

Introduction

I wrote the first edition of this book in the mid '90s when I moved my mother from her home in Boston to Northern Virginia where my husband and I were living at the time. After she passed away, I shelved the project. The emotional roller coaster of dealing with the move, transitioning from just the daughter to the "dutiful daughter" and caregiver, and Mom's physical decline and death were too raw. I did not want to relive the experience at book signings and speeches.

In 2008, my husband Dick and I relocated to Manhattan. In 2010, after a 30+ career in the nonprofit and public sectors, we both got our real estate licenses and joined Prudential Douglas Elliman. After renting for a couple of years to test out a couple of neighborhoods, we decided to buy a coop. We bought our apartment as an "estate sale" creating a new knowledge base developed from this transaction which had many challenges and many benefits. The challenges included the need for a total gut renovation – in a Manhattan coop – a very complicated process. The major benefit was that we got a fabulous buy from heirs who were eager to sell the property.

We realized that our personal experience in moving a parent as well as ourselves can benefit many of our fellow baby boomers and others who are downsizing themselves, relocating or dealing with the relocation of a loved one. This is a new sandwich generation, many of my friends are still dealing with kids at home or in college while dealing with the issues of parents needing to downsize or move closer to their caregivers. In my own case, my husband Dick and I learned many lessons from moving my mother that we have applied to our own situation as we have adjusted our living arrangements to match up with our changing lifestyle. We did not get it right the first time – we have moved seven times in ten years.

One of the biggest decisions for us or our parents is the sale of the family home, be it a coop in Manhattan or a cottage on Cape Cod. The issue is a delicate one for all involved and the decision has significant financial implications for both the parent and the caregivers – usually the children. If one or both parents have passed away, and heirs are faced with selling from an estate, new issues and challenges are in place that must be addressed.

So, I dusted off my manuscript and updated it to deal with the changes that have come about in the last decade that impact our knowledge of aging issues as well as ways to help our loved ones make some of the most difficult decisions of their lives. I have pared it down as well and included anecdotes from my own story and those of my friends. I have included some check lists and spread sheets and made suggestions for putting together your own worksheets to use as you proceed along the road. I hope that this guide helps you and your parent.

My Story

My mother had her first heart attack the night before she boarded a plane to attend her grandson's graduation from William & Mary. Alone in her apartment, she passed out after ignoring warning signs that included nausea and a severe headache. As a matter of fact, women are frequently unaware that their symptoms are different from those of men and do not necessarily include the widely accepted symptoms of either chest pain or shooting pain down the arm.

Eventually she regained consciousness, finished packing and arrived at the airport in time for her flight from Boston, Massachusetts to Northern Virginia, home to her two children, six grandchildren and an ever increasing number of adorable great-grandchildren.

Her second heart attack was a repeat performance, coming in tandem with a January visit to Virginia to escape an especially harsh New England winter.

My brother Howard and I knew that Mom could no longer live alone. She would have to move closer to her support network - her children. After much debate and cajoling, Mom agreed to move -- a brave and life-changing decision forcing her to give up a large chunk of her independence and shouldering Howard and me with new, as yet undefined responsibilities.

While each of us understood that Mom could not maneuver this move on her own, it became clear over the next several months that none of us had any idea what the move would entail and how ill-prepared we were for this daunting task. Mom expected that I, her only daughter, would be the one to "hold her hand" - pack the boxes and make the arrangements. It would never have occurred to her that her son would take time off from work to run errands and explore the lower reaches of the basement storage room.

That was 15 years ago and today men are increasingly assuming responsibilities, not just as engaged parents of their own children, but for their aging parents as well. And many of us, who have entered and stayed in the workforce, do not have the time to manage our own moves, much less those of our parents or elderly relatives.

With no manuals or guidebooks to tell us what to do or even what to expect from this experience, I solicited the advice of friends and colleagues many of whom were facing the problem of moving or caring for an elderly parent. For most, the problem was magnified by the distance from home our careers had taken us. While they were empathetic and quick to share the pitfalls and wisdom they had gained in relocating a parent, their experiences were just a window on the obstacles which would be faced at each step in Mom's move. I had no idea that the personal challenge I faced was a growing concern, not only to individuals, but to the companies that employ them and the communities in which they live. Later in this volume, Ph.D. Lori Sokol advises us on the emotional stress we as caregivers face, not just the emotional stress on the parent.

When I first approached the problem, I thought that there was no information available to help in my task. What I have since discovered is that there is a great deal of information, and many resources are now available to provide care at all levels to our senior population. This guide was written to "capture" what I learned the hard way - through experience and many mistakes, so that future caregivers can have a road map to follow in this important but confusing process. But don't stop here, you can find many solutions in your hometown or neighborhood by exploring the web or visiting the websites of the organizations referenced after each chapter.

While the team that contributed to the Guide cannot solve all of your problems, we can help direct you to community resources that are available to assist you and your parents with many important issues – insurance, elder care, and more. And now that Dick and I are in the real estate field, we can direct you to professionals who can help with the relocation of a parent, friend or loved one, the sale of the family home or the purchase of a condo in an assisted living facility. We would be happy to refer you to an agent sensitive to senior issues anywhere in the country through the

Prudential Douglas Elliman referral network. It generally takes a team of brokers, attorneys, financial advisors and even stagers, contractors and movers to put the move on the right track, reduce stress for all, and find the right solution for parent and child.

Chapter One

First Steps

Was there ever a time when women stayed at home and oversaw the smooth flow of a household of three generations? Did parents of another generation spend their golden years in the warm glow of a loving family? If it ever existed, and I am sure it did for some, this warm and loving picture does not capture the reality of my life or the lives of other women and men whose careers and responsibilities require that they work outside of the home. My generation - baby boomers as we have been called in the media all our lives, has seen women enter the work force in record numbers. Through both opportunity and necessity, our lives have changed from the homemaker experience of our mothers. Whether or not we would want to elect the option, most of us are not able to give up our careers and stay home to provide the support today's elderly require. The need to care for a loved one can and probably will happen to you, if it has not already. Andrew Scharlach, professor of Social Welfare at the University of California at Berkeley says that by the year 2020, one in three adults will have elder-care responsibilities. Americans are living longer; the 85+ population is the fasting growing age group in the country. Even Willard Scott has raised the age of his Schmucker's Birthday tributes on the Today Show. Reaching 100 is no longer amazing. But increased longevity also means, for many of our older citizens, the need for some sort of support - physical or financial or both for an increasingly longer period of time. According to the American Association of Retired People (AARP), seven million Americans provide help to a relative in some way on any given day. AARP's statistics on elder care date back to the early eighties when 70% of caregivers were female. More than half the caregivers continue to work in full or part-time jobs and many also care for school-age children. Just as the record number of women entering the workforce 20 years ago revolutionized the child care industry, so too is it changing the face of eldercare as the needs of two career families' impact on the nature of the solutions available to deal with older parents. But the solutions to assist in each unique situation are different from state to state and community to community. Much responsibility falls to the individual to ferret out information on adult day care, home health aides, long-term care insurance, meals-on-wheels and other programs to improve the quality of life of today's senior population.

Take Action

During your next visit home:
1. Identify Resources in the Community
2. Enlist Neighbors and Friends for Support
3. Make an Emergency Telephone Numbers List.
4. Make a List of Medical Information

Before you even have a discussion with your parent or elderly relative about the options available and desirable in your particular situation, there are actions you can and should take to "stabilize" the situation and begin a transition to care giving.

The Simple Things Mean A Lot

If you are reading this guide, you have probably already decided that your parents are in need of additional attention and assistance either now or in the near future. These simple things can provide both you and your loved one with an immediate sense of increased involvement and security. If your parent lives at a distance, or if you travel a great deal, you should make an **"emergency telephone number list"**. You can do this over the telephone or by email even before you make your next visit. Keep one copy beside your phone and another in your wallet. This will enable you to respond to a telephone appeal from your parent or emergency medical personnel if he or she has been injured or is ill or if you are unable to reach her/him by telephone. You need to be able to contact a neighbor, a doctor, the local hospital and an ambulance service. It is a good idea to make arrangements to have a neighbor check periodically on your parent to make certain that he/she is doing all right. In my Mom's independent living condominium they had a buddy system. If Mom's "buddy" saw that a newspaper had not been removed from in front of the door by noon each day, she would check to make certain Mom was O.K. You can make these arrangements in your condo, coop or neighborhood. The neighbor would, of course, need to have a key to the home and your parent will have to agree to this arrangement. Don't forget to add the security code to the alarm system to your emergency phone list. If you have identified a buddy, that person should have a front door key as well as the access code for the alarm.

Even if the problem is temporary and seemingly minor, you can provide a great deal of help and comfort, even from a distance. A mild cold or stomach upset could keep an elderly relative from a routine visit to the grocery store. As many of the elderly develop poor nutrition habits, lack of readily available fresh food could turn a minor medical problem into a serious one. Here in New York City, this is never a problem as everyone delivers. If your parents live elsewhere, you will need to do the research and check with the markets in the neighborhood to find out which will deliver. My Mom's refrigerator generally contained very little in the way of long term provisions. In her eighties, managing heavy bundles was difficult. In addition, a visit to the local market had become part of the daily socialization ritual. A sudden snow storm could keep Mom in doors alone for days at a time. Knowing that the market would deliver took a load off my mind.

Delivery of routine and special medications is also important, so check to make certain that a local pharmacy will either deliver or use a taxi to transport medications during a period when your loved one is homebound. Here in Manhattan, this goes without saying, but if your loved one is in a small town, you may have to do some research. On your next visit home, make plans to visit your parent's primary care physician and ask that you be notified of any serious medical problems that come to his or her attention. If this is not possible, most doctors will talk with you on the phone, especially if your parent has laid the ground work. A little advance preparation can ease your mind when you are far away. And **urge** your parent to call "911" in an emergency.

These simple tasks will provide you with a great deal of peace of mind.

Recommended Reading:

"Miles Away & Still Caring: A Guide for Long-Distance Caregivers", AARP.org

Other Resources:

The *"Eldercare Locator"* is a public service of the U.S. Administration on Aging. The service is administered by the National Association of Area Agencies on Aging and the National Association of State Units on Aging. The locator, which is staffed from 9:00 a.m. until 11:00 p.m. Eastern Time, will help you to find a range of services available throughout the country. Have the county and/or city name and zip code in the area for which you want information and be able to succinctly define the problem you are trying to resolve. 1-(800)-677-1117 or http://www.eldercare.gov/Eldercare. NET/Public/Index.aspx.

HELPFUL HINTS

Emergency Phone List

Include numbers and email for:

- Neighbor
- Primary Care Physician
- Pharmacy
- Ambulance Service
- Hospital
- Taxi service
- Local Grocery Store

Chapter Two

Developing the Plan

Now that you have initiated interim steps for involvement in your parent's life/health management, you can begin to address both a time frame and a plan for a long-term solution. As I have stated before, this guide is for those of us who must or want to keep our jobs and who need help in caring for our parents. If necessary, as was the case for Howie and myself, we moved our mother to the community in which we both lived. This was easier for us, although much more difficult for my mother. But it was a decision arrived at after much thought, examining alternatives, and analyzing financial requirements, health benefits and costs and other personal issues.

Examine the Alternatives

There are hundreds of scenarios that can bring us face to face with a new relationship with our parents - the role of caregiver. Each situation is different. For some, the role reversal - becoming our parents' parent - is a slow process, as mine was, gradually increasing responsibilities over a number of years; or the responsibility can come all once.

Some must deal with the debilitating effects of Alzheimer's or other forms of dementia more common in the elderly population or with dealing with both aging parents at the same time or in close succession. Americans are living longer and are, for the most part staying healthier than any previous generation. Even a healthy, independent parent frequently needs increased attention if not assistance as the years go by. Recently, a friend's father became seriously ill and the mother was suffering from stress and depression. Just one problem was that she had never managed the family's finances. Until the kids stepped in to help her get a grasp on checking bank balances and paying bills on time, their health insurance nearly lapsed as the bill had not been paid in four months.

The death of a spouse is certainly a defining moment in this journey. Even if the surviving spouse is healthy, as described above he or she may not know how to assume the new responsibilities that had been handled or shared by the deceased. This could be as mundane as taking out the garbage on trash pick-up day to preparing the income tax return. The place in the life of a mother or father of their deceased spouse cannot be filled by a child or other caretaker, but a loved one can help to stave off the debilitating effects of loneliness by providing company and comfort. At a distance, this is more difficult than if you lived in the same community, but increased telephone contact and visits back and forth at increased frequency are probably to be expected.

Examine Financial Requirements

As the needs increase, we each must determine how to deal with the needs of our elderly parents without total disruption of our own lives. For some this means giving up a job or taking a leave of absence to provide care personally. The financial implications of these decisions to you and your family are substantial and must be taken into consideration when planning a move or interim assistance.

When my father was dying, I made more than 14 trips over a five month period between Washington, D.C. and Boston. On three occasions I flew to Boston not knowing whether he would make it through the day. Dad's condition was up and down so many times that I never knew when I left to return home to work, whether I would ever see him again. I felt guilty leaving my Mother alone to deal with the medical decisions and other problems while I, at least, had respite from the stress of the hospital during my interim work life and social life at home in Washington.

After his death, my responsibilities to my mother were more difficult to define. When did she need me? What was a critical situation? When do I get on the plane and go help? How is she doing, really, when you haven't seen her in person for more than three months? I didn't know the answers to these questions and did not know where to go to get help. I didn't even know that there were places to which I could turn. Today, a web cam on a local computer or Skype can help stay in touch visually and are reasonably priced stop-gaps to the in-person visit. If the parent is not tech savvy, a neighbor's child or an intern from a local high school or college can be engaged to help out.

There are books which address the issues faced by primary caregivers and which address the physical, physiological and psychological aspects of that role. There are also both government-sponsored and private resources in most communities. One friend whose parent lived in Northern Virginia turned to the "Ombudsman for the Aging" of Fairfax County, Virginia to assist her. He was able to provide information on which nursing homes had been "decertified" by Medicare, what adult day care programs in the area received favorable reviews, and where she could find a psychologist who specialized in the depression problems frequently facing the elderly. There are also Agencies on Aging in most states and many communities.

Analyze Your Personal Situation

We decided that Mom could no longer live alone in the apartment she had called home for more than 40 years. There was no garage either in the home or neighborhood and parking on the street was difficult. If she went out after 4:00 o'clock in the afternoon, she could not be guaranteed a parking space when she returned. That meant walking on uneven sidewalks in a hilly neighborhood. As Mom's arthritis in her knees and hips was beginning to seriously interfere with her mobility, the lack of adequate parking was an increasingly serious problem. Honestly, we really did not think she should be driving at all. She was living in a rental apartment that was greatly in need of expensive updating: the plumbing was old and unreliable, the paint was chipped, carpets worn and appliances out of date. In addition, her washing machine was not easily accessible. Much of her generation, both family and friends had died and those who remained, while as helpful as they could be within the limits of their own resources and demands of their own jobs and families, could not provide an adequate support network.

One alternative we considered briefly was to hire a companion for my mother who could keep an eye on her to make sure she was O.K. and who could help with shopping and housekeeping chores. One summer I tried to hire a couple of college girls to live with Mom and help with housekeeping and shopping at her summer cottage. The previous summer

Mom had slipped on a wet flagstone in the yard and broken her collar bone. Fortunately, my niece and a friend were with her at the time and stayed on for the rest of the summer. They helped Mom get dressed. Because she could not drive until the bone was healed, they took her on errands and to the grocery store. The arrangement worked well for Mom although it was not a very fun summer for the girls.

The following spring I flew home to Boston to interview candidates for summer help. I lined up several and picked out a lovely young woman who came with good recommendations. As was true the prior year with my niece, I allowed her to bring a friend to keep her company. The arrangement did not even last a month. Mom did not like having "strangers" in the house. I asked if there was a friend or relative she would like to have stay with her but she said "no". So a live in companion was out of the question. Mother did not want a stranger in her house and there was no likely non-stranger to fill the role. Her reaction was not unusual. In her article "Elder Care at Work", (Working Woman, June, 1995), Julia Lawlor reported that "Remington Products announced a pilot program in 1989 to pay half the cost of hiring a professional home-health aide to watch employees' older relatives when caregivers needed a break. Yet no one used the program, although many employees at the Bridgeport, Connecticut shaving products firm had elder-care responsibilities. Spokeswoman Cynthia Uhlan says "...the company discovered that employees' parents objected to having strangers in their homes, preferring to have neighbors or friends watch them instead. The program was eliminated."

> ### Take Action
> ---
> 1. Determine whether a companion is needed
> 2. Discuss level of need
> 3. Create a draft schedule

But this approach does work for some, especially if the need is temporary, such as a broken bone. The degree of assistance provided by a companion can vary and the qualifications of the person chosen will depend on the need. If companionship for part of the day and occasional shopping assistance is all that is needed, little or no training or experience is needed. If medical support and personal hygiene assistance are required, then the experience level will be more important.

A sample companion interview and suggestions for an application follow. If you create an application form, be sure to include personal contact information, work history (including volunteer activities) and detailed contact information for references. If you plan on checking the candidates credit history, you should advise them of this in advance and request their social security number. Alternatively, you can ask them to purchase a copy of their credit history and provide you with a copy.

After they have completed the application, either in your presence or by email or letter, prepare yourself with the questions you will ask during the interview.

Helpful Hints

Include in the Application
- Date
- **Personal Information**
  - Name
  - Address
  - Daytime and Evening phone
  - Email
  - Date of birth
  - Social Security Number (to check credit history)
  - Referred by/contact info
- **Work History**
  - Dates of employment
  - Position
  - Employer
  - Supervisor
  - Employer Phone/email
  - Duties
  - Reason for leaving:

Interview Questions

- Have you ever worked as a companion before?
    - If yes, When?
    - Why did that position end?
    - Can I call the person/relative for a reference?
        - Name:
        - Phone Number:
        - Best time to call:

- Have you cared for or assisted in the care of an elderly or sick parent or relative?
    - If yes, please describe the circumstances.
- Have you performed volunteer work which brought you in contact with the elderly?
    - Please explain.
    - Did you enjoy it? What were the greatest rewards? What did you like the least about the experience?

- Have you taken classes at the college level which deal with the problems and needs of the elderly? What were they? How do you think they would apply to this situation?

- What are the demands of your personal schedule? (school commitments, family, social, other employment)

- How much time each day do you envision your companion commitment will consume?

- Would you be happy/comfortable assisting with personal hygiene requirements such as dressing and bathing?

- Would you be happy to sit and watch television, play cards or talk for several hours each day or evening?

- Would you take Mom shopping
    for groceries?
    for clothing?

- Would you take Mom to the movies, museums or sports events?

- Would you accompany Mom on scheduled visits to the Doctor?

- Do you have a cell phone where you can be reached in emergency situations?

- What are some things you would <u>not</u> want to be responsible for?

- Would your friends/relatives describe you as a patient person?

- Have you ever had to deal with an emergency situation?
    Please describe the event:

    Please describe the actions you took:

    What was the outcome?

- Do you drive a car?

- Other:

    NOTES:

Whatever the level of need, an application is a good idea. Going through the questions above and adding your own will help you to focus on the need. It will also clarify for both you and the companion exactly what the responsibilities and expectations are so that there will not be confusion or disappointment at a later date. It is also a good idea to develop a job description. From the job description, you can then develop a simple advertisement to place on a community bulletin board, in a college newspaper, posted on craigslist or in the local newspaper.

JOB DESCRIPTION/WANT AD

Seeking a part-time companion for an elderly woman in good health. Four hours daily from 10:00 a.m. to 2:00 p.m., Monday through Saturday. Prepare light lunch; assist with shopping or other outings on foot or by car. Occasional additional hours available. Must be able to drive a car. Experience caring for or exposure to the elderly preferred. $15 per hour. Please fax cover letter and resume to: ( )   .

Chapter Three

Timing - When is the Right time?

If either my brother or I lived in the community, my mother could probably have remained in her own home for a longer period of time. If we could come by a couple of times a week to check on her, if we were around to be called in an emergency, the urgency of her move would not have been as great. But we both worked in the Washington metropolitan area and had established careers and homes in that community and our mother lived in Boston.

We briefly examined the possibility of moving Mom to a different apartment that had garage parking, was on the street car line and near shopping and doctors. We also looked at independent living facilities, senior residence communities and such in the Boston area. These would not solve the problem, however, of our personal desire to be involved in our mother's daily life and to make certain that she was healthy, happy and receiving the support she needed. We finally came to the conclusion that if Mom was to move out of her home and sell our beach house, we figured that the best alternative was to make a clean break and move closer to or with us. My brother Howard (Howie) and I are both very fortunate to have spouses that got along very well with their Mother-in-law and we each offered our homes as a temporary or permanent option.

Maintaining Independence/Infusing Support

Mom made clear immediately that while she loved us all, she wanted her own place. A recent television feature showcased an Orlando, Florida builder who had developed a floor plan that included a mother-in law suite with its own private entrance, handicap accessible en suite bath and a large bedroom/study. Even in a challenging real estate market in one of the most challenged states, the properties were being snapped up by families looking to care for a parent but who wanted to maintain the privacy of each.

Mom's first thought was that she would rent an apartment near one of us and continue to drive and take care of herself. In other words, she would take the life she was living in Boston and merely transplant it to Virginia. Had she been younger or stronger this might have been a viable option. It was a lesson learned and we now advise friends that it is best for parents to relocate while they are still in good health with good mobility. One of my friends recently convinced his parents to move from their Southern home to Manhattan. They adjusted immediately and are enjoying the museums, classes and discount tickets available throughout the city to "seniors". Had my Mom moved ten years earlier, soon after my Dad's death, independent living might have worked for at least a while. Her first reaction to

HELPFUL HINTS

If you are not completely familiar with the available options in your community, your best choice is to work with a real estate professional. It is our job to know the inventory and to provide you with options at every price point whether you are going to purchase or rent. And the best news is that it does not cost you or your loved one anything. The buyer's agent receives compensation from the seller. My firm, Prudential Douglas Elliman has a global network of agents who are the best in the business.

In Manhattan, I can work with you directly. Not in the city? Let me refer you to one of my colleagues in the Prudential network.

senior residences or other organized facilities was that she did not want to be around a lot of "old people". I pointed out to her that if she moved into an apartment, all her neighbors would go to work each day and that she would be alone and lonely, one of the conditions we were trying to remedy. We also were quite convinced that Mom should no longer be driving and that when she moved to Virginia we would find a way of convincing her not to drive any more.

It was difficult to get beyond Mom's preconception of what an independent living facility was like. She envisioned people in wheel chairs with blank stares warehoused and waiting to be fed. On her first "trial" look-see at what might be available in the area, she refused to even go in and look at the upscale, then new Jefferson Senior Residence in Ballston, Virginia. It had been recommended highly by several of my friends, but Mom resisted. Ultimately, this is where she bought and where she happily and actively lived for four years until her death. There is no doubt in our minds that the move greatly improved the quality of her life in the last years of her life. It takes time to ease into the idea that life as you knew it is about to change forever. This is true on both sides of the equation. From my perspective, I can say that Mom's move to Virginia greatly enriched my life as well as hers.

No one defining incident will tell you that the time has come - for you or for your loved one. It is a process that you both must work through and that process will include your siblings, spouse and children. This might be considered your "caregiver group" and it might also be appropriate to add a member of the clergy or a physician. You need to determine how much care is needed and how much care are you prepared to personally give? Preparation means many things from preparing yourself emotionally for the new responsibilities you are about to undertake, to renovating your home to accommodate the needs of an elderly parent, to finding time in your day to make a phone call, run an errand, or pay a visit. How much independence can your loved one still manage and for how long? While some of these are quantifiable and can be examined objectively, the most important and elusive is coming to grips with the decision itself and saying, yes the time has come. For most people, the process will take time and the extent of care will gradually build. My father's death took its toll on my mother's health.

Take Action

1. Convene your caregiver group
2. Examine new information
3. Share information on financial requirements
4. Review your options

Not only is it psychologically difficult for any person to watch her love and partner of more than 50 years die, his prolonged hospitalization created physical demands that taxed the body as well as the soul. Walking the long, hard corridors of Massachusetts General Hospital for six months, sitting in waiting rooms for surgeries to end, sitting alongside a quiet bed for hours, days and months on end drained her spirit and physical resources. By the time the Doctors called us early one November day to come in and say our goodbyes as Dad was slipping away, Mom had a raging case of sciatica and had to be wheeled to his room.

Howard and I knew that it would take time for her to "recover" from this passage and that a move at that time would have only added one trauma on top of another. In the back of our minds, however, we both knew that the time would come when Mom would have to move.

From the beginning, we had to step in to fill the unfillable void. The summer house had to be opened, a task that had been my father's domain. Each spring my husband and I flew or drove north and handled the taking down of storm windows, reconnecting water and electric services, bagging leaves, trimming hedges and the other myriad tasks that accompany home ownership. In the fall, we would return to reverse the process and take down the screens, put up the storm windows and ready the house for the winter. Each March I flew to Boston to prepare her tax returns. It would have been cheaper to hire an accountant, but Mom wanted me. Not only was the financial burden of these little trips difficult, it was using up all my leave from work. After spending all my "vacation" time addressing Mom's priorities, there was little left for my husband or myself.

Long before my father's death, because it was difficult (and expensive) for all of us now living in Virginia to travel North for holidays, Mom and Dad came South to celebrate or merely to visit. This pattern continued after Dad's death. As the years went by, it became increasingly difficult for my mother to make the trip by herself. Her anxiety level was always high. Hating to spend money on a cab, she would ask my cousin or her younger sister to drive her to or from the airport. But they each ran businesses and it was not always possible for them to adjust their schedules to Mom's demands. After one trip home from the airport in a cab, she discovered that she didn't have her house key and she sat for three hours on a cold porch waiting for her neighbor to return home and let her in. Merely packing a suitcase and getting it to the front door for the cab driver was physically taxing.

In icy weather she couldn't always get out to the store. Her physical agility never returned after her fall and with each year she became increasingly less confident on stairs and curbs. I worried about her just getting in and out of the house. Her washing machine was down a flight of rickety stairs that ended on a hard concrete surface. She parked her car on the street and frequently could not find a parking space close to the house. I worried about her all the time.

Mom always sounded great on the phone. I could listen to her voice and picture my mother of ten or twenty years earlier. But when I saw her, so small and frail, it broke my heart to leave her on her own to fend for herself.

And, much to our consternation, she continued to drive. All summer long she drove the 85 miles of mostly highway back and forth from Boston to our home on Cape Cod. She didn't trust the Post Office to adequately forward her mail so she returned home once a week to collect it. Never a good driver, I worried constantly that she would be in an accident.

During one visit to Boston, Dick noticed a new dent on her car. Mom admitted to driving too close to and side swiping a parked truck. She didn't even leave a note for the poor truck driver because she was "angry that he had parked in the wrong place." My poor father, who had been in the insurance industry his entire life, must have been spinning in his grave.

The issue escalated when during one of our trips to Boston. Mom was supposed to pick Dick and me up at Logan Airport and we were to meet her curbside at the USAir terminal. The plane was on time and we expected to see Mom as we exited the terminal building. She wasn't there. As the minutes slowly passed we began to worry. After 15 minutes I called her house to see if she had forgotten our time of arrival. There was no answer. The weather was clear and our flight had arrived mid-day so we did not think that traffic was a problem. Of course, there could have been an accident and travel through the Callaghan tunnel from Boston to the airport could never be predicted. After an hour had passed we did not know what to do. Do we call the police to see if she has been in an accident? Do we call a friend to see if the car is at the house indicating that she might still be inside and in trouble? All sorts of evil scenarios went through our minds during that long hour. A check with the taxi dispatcher told us that there were no special traffic tie ups reported in the city. We had just decided that one of us would cab to her apartment in Brighton, the other remaining at the airport in case Mom arrived, when the car appeared over the hill, Mom's head barely visible over the steering wheel. She had gotten lost in the airport and had been circling for over an hour trying to remember what the signs meant and which ramp to take. We were all upset. Mom would not admit that her driving ability was diminished and said it could happen to anyone. But she had been coming to this airport for years and had picked us up or dropped us off on numerous occasions without difficulty. Dick and I knew that in the future, we would take the train and subway from the airport- adding an additional hour to our trip. But the most upsetting aspect was our having to face the fact that Mom's capacity to live independently was diminishing.

But we were not yet prepared to face the larger issue of when to insist that Mom stop driving. This is a big issue and nearly every person I interviewed for this book raised the problem. The Alzheimer's Association provides a list of "warning signs" of unsafe driving.

> ## Take Action
>
> ### Analyze Warning Signs
>
> 1. Is unable to locate familiar places
> 2. Does not observe traffic signs or drives at an inappropriate speed
> 3. Makes poor or slow decisions in traffic
> 4. Becomes angry, frustrated or confused while driving.

But (like me), Mom was always stubborn and she greatly valued her freedom. Mom knew that Howie and I did not want her to drive anymore and that moving to Virginia meant giving up that symbol of her freedom. Mom continued to drive both locally and to her home on Cape Cod for two more years. I think we are all very lucky that she did not have a serious accident injuring either herself or anyone else. Howie and I insisted when Mom moved to Virginia that she give up driving and Howie bought her car from her. I am embarrassed to say that we prevailed through intimidation. We pointed out that she could not drive on her Massachusetts license and would have to take both a written and driving test in Virginia. Always concerned about money and loathe to spend, we tried to explain, to little or no avail, the favorable economic consequences of not owning a car. In addition to the cash provided by the sale, we estimated for her the huge annual savings in insurance costs, gas and repairs. The resulting sum was more than enough to pay for cabs whenever she might want to take one. But she still only took a cab under great duress and stayed home rather than employ that mode of transportation. She pointed out on every available occasion to anyone who would listen the number of people in her building who still - at age 90 or more - drove their own cars.

One day when I was leaving her building a shriveled old woman entered the elevator, hunched over and examined at a range of about an inch and a half, the buttons on the elevator wall. After pressing one, she asked me if she had pressed "P2" for the parking garage and I affirmed that it was pressed. When that floor arrived, she took her car keys and prepared to drive away! I was glad to be safe inside the building.

Whether local or long distance, the lack of mobility creates new demands that you will have to deal with sooner or later. It seems a small thing, but the loss of the car is a loss of independence and can cause depression. It is important that the "issue" of transportation be minimized.

By the fall of 1993, we were all moving toward the decision. After her two travel related heart attacks we knew the time had come. During our visits to the Cape over the years, my husband, Dick, and I would ask her when she wanted to move south. Her response for several years was "I know that eventually I will have to move, but I am not ready yet." When asked to define what would make her "ready", she was unable to tell us, articulating only that she knew that she would need more and more help as the years progressed. In January, 1994, she finally agreed that she needed help and that the time had come to move.

Making the Decision to Move Forward

For my friend Judy, the founder and CEO of a large furniture company, her mother never reached that point of acceptance. "She never agreed, I had to take action. Control is her biggest problem. I think the biggest fear for the elderly is losing control. I think it devastated her when I told her I was going to take control [of her finances]. She didn't hand it over to me easily. It took me quite a long period of time to have her sign any documents that would give my any ability - a power of attorney - to deal with things for her."

To get her mother to agree to a move into an independent living facility, Judy says "I had to spend a year letting her fail. I had to let things fall down. She is too strong. I remember the comments when I told her I was going to start paying the bills. She said I was 'selling her down the river'. I loved that comment. It was the last thing I wanted to do - any of this. And none of my sisters wanted any part of it. My mother is very difficult to manage. She had done a brilliant job of managing her own money since my father died. When I looked at the record keeping she did - she was far superior to any of her children, so it must have been an enormously painful experience for her the day she had to hand it over to me."

But Judy says that the primary issue necessitating moving her mother into an independent living facility was her health. "She couldn't take care of herself. She was forgetting to take medicine...We had her checked for Alzheimer's and she doesn't have that, she has a mild form of dementia." Added to this is the isolation experienced by many surviving spouses whose lives have focused on another person no longer there. Judy believes "The problem is loneliness; it was really the biggest indicator that I needed to do something. I remember I walked into her town house and all the shades were pulled down. It was a bright, sunny September day, but the room was absolutely pitch dark. It had a depressing quality about it. It was unkempt. My mother had always been meticulously clean and neat. And that's when I realized something was wrong." Although Judy is the middle of two other sisters, the responsibility fell to her to make the decision and execute the plan. "It fell to me for a couple of reasons. One, my mother is so impressed and intrigued with my business...My older sister is quite capable, but she lives in St. Louis. Her accomplishments were going unnoticed by my mother because she wasn't around. So my mother took all her fears and terrors and figured that if I could run a business, I could probably manage her life."

A health crisis brings the issue front and center, but even then evaluation is called for. Is the problem temporary, as was my Mom's broken collar bone, or is it a symptom of increased dependency? A visit with the primary care physician will help you to understand the parent's situation, but it is only one piece of the puzzle, not the total answer. It is important that the doctor understand the family's position and know what situation the person will move into as well as out of. After two heart attacks, my mother's cardiologist was justifiably concerned about the effect of the stress of a move on Mom's heart. It was important for him to know that family would work hard to minimize that stress and that Mom's life - her social interaction, exercise, and nutrition would all improve in her new situation.

Take Action: Conduct a Reality Check

Reality Check List

- Does he/she still drive a car?
  - Have there been any accidents?
  - Is he/she able to locate familiar places?
  - Does he/she observe traffic signs?
  - Does he/she drive at an inappropriate speed?
  - Does he/she make poor or slow decisions in traffic?
  - Does he/she become angry, frustrated or confused while driving?
- Is he/she able to monitor and administer medications?
  - Does he/she take medicines in appropriate, recommended doses?
  - Are medications taken at the prescribed times?
  - Has he/she ever forgotten to take required medications in a timely manner?
  - Has he/she ever taken a double dose of medication because he/she could not remember having already taken the drug?
  - Does arthritis or palsy in the hands make administering drugs difficult?
- Has his/her physical agility diminished?
  - Has there been a fall resulting in a broken bone, sprain or bruising?
  - Are stairs or other physical barriers in the home becoming a problem?
- Is he/she providing for himself/herself proper nutrition either by cooking or eating out?
- Does he/she get out of the house regularly and maintain an active social life?
- Have his/her personal hygiene habits changed for the worse?
- Is he/she able to keep the home clean and neat?

- Are bills paid on time?
- Does he/she remember and keep appointments?
- Is short term memory diminishing?

Chapter Four

Taking Stock

Before selecting a new living arrangement, it is important to determine what services will your loved one need tomorrow, next month, or next year. At best, moving is traumatic for your parent and for you and long as well as short-range objectives should be considered before you begin. Believe me, you do not want to have to do this again in six months because you have selected an inflexible or inappropriate option. The decision as to where to go and when should involve doctors and other care providers in the home community as well as in the new community. These visits or calls will help to minimize mistakes.

Independent or Assisted Living?

Considerations in services available include the elder's required assistance in meal preparation, personal grooming, physical therapy, house cleaning, grocery shopping, administering medication, transportation, entertainment, physical activity, psychological counseling, paying bills and medical attention. These are just a sampling of what professionals describe as the possible 300 combinations of services the parent may need over time. Overlaid on this problem is the ever present financial consideration of what you can afford. A range of living arrangements are available, depending on your location and the degree of assistance required. Several terms are now in common usage and can be confusing - "assisted living" and "independent living" are generally applied to residential communities which provide a range of services for those elders who do not need 24-hour care or supervision. The cost and relative "luxury" of this form of housing varies and generally depends on location, amenities and the size of the individual's own home within the community - whether it is one room or a full apartment. Some services are included in most assisted living arrangements with additional services available at increased charges. For example, my mother's condo fee included a weekly housekeeping visit. It was important to me that this be an included, rather than an optional charge. Mom, whose eyesight had deteriorated, did not see the dust and improperly washed utensils and would not have voluntarily agreed to a weekly expense to keep her apartment clean. But without this service, her apartment would be a mess. Despite her good intentions, she did not have the stamina to change the sheets on her double bed, wash and fold them, vacuum or wash bathroom and kitchen floors. Even had she lived here in New York with our access to home delivery and wash and fold, it would have been more than she could have handled on her own. The brief but thorough weekly visit kept her apartment sparkling and she was proud of its appearance.

Take Action

Expand your Caregiver Group

1. Confer with current physicians
2. Get referrals to new medical resources in new community
3. Contact physicians and caregiver organizations in new community

Judy says that the health care provisions in her home state of Massachusetts - Medex (a medigap plan) combined with Medicaid, provided her mother with a daily visit from a home health care nurse, supplementing the assistance provided by her residential community. "Because of some heart problems - she had two minor heart attacks; I was able to get a health care nurse to come in every day. She makes certain that my mother starts the day off with breakfast, helps her pick up a little bit, any food shopping she wants - it's a miracle." While the senior "independent living" facility in which she lives will take residents shopping, each service carries with it a separate charge. Judy says, "I couldn't have afforded it."

Until her declining health required a nursing home, my friend Betty 's Mom visited the nurse practitioner at her assisted living community for her daily medications. Her two bedroom apartment was a rental and included many of the amenities of the condominium independent and assisted living facilities.

My Mom lived independently until her death at age 87 though for the last three months of her life she had a live in care provider. She had a dread of dying in a hospital attached to machines and bottles. It continues to give me satisfaction that on the last day of her life, my son visited her in the afternoon for a nice chat, she went to dinner in the communal dining hall with her friends, and quietly passed away in her own apartment watching her favorite TV program – *Jeopardy.*

For many people, the need to move a parent occurs when he or she is no longer able to live independently. If they need 24-hour care or supervision throughout the day, then a nursing home is probably the solution. The **American Association of Homes and Services for the Aging** provides free information on how to evaluate nursing homes. Many nursing homes are nonprofit and are run by religious denominations and are administered by professional staff who report to a Board of Directors or Trustees.

info@aahsa.org; www.aahsa.org/

2519 Connecticut Avenue, NW Washington, DC 20008-1520

202-783-2242 (Voice) 202-783-2255 (FAX)

Online Resources

Finding the Right Aging Services http://www.aahsa.org/choice.aspx

Homes and Services Directory for Older Adults http://www.aahsa.org/section.aspx?id=280

Take Action: Conduct a Needs Assessment

Use the ideas in this chapter to create a needs assessment. Have a column for each issue for which help is needed and one to check for today, soon or someday. Include:

- Transportation
- Taking Medication
- Grooming and Hygiene
- Dressing
- Managing Finances
  - Bill Payment
  - Taxes
  - Insurance Filings
- Meal Preparation
- Social Activities

Chapter Five

Examining the Alternatives

Before getting one's heart set on a specific senior assisted living residence or nursing home, or deciding to take a parent into one's own home, the specific financial capability of the parent alone or with the help of children or siblings must be fully understood. It is necessary to analyze both financial and physical resources - the parent's and your own, which can be applied to the move and new life style. You must begin by understanding what it will cost. If your parent(s) own real estate, the first, and often the most difficult decision is to sell the current home.

Legal aspects of selling real estate

Matt Abrams is an attorney with Russo and Burke in Manhattan and contributes the following advice:

In my experience, the issues involved in selling a house owned by an elderly parent fall into four categories:

(1) authority – who signs the papers, affidavit, tax forms, etc.;
(2) money – what price under what conditions, adjustments to the price between contract and closing, mortgage payoffs, legal fees, brokers' commissions, and taxes;
(3) issues with marketable title; and
(4) assorted practical considerations relating to the contract and closing.

Issues of authority most commonly appear when a parent's ability to think and act for himself or herself is beginning to slip. State law governs what documents can successfully give one person power over another's financial affairs, and most attorneys in practice can prepare a Durable Power of Attorney ("POA") document without difficulty. The "donor" or "principal" of the power – the parent – must be able to understand the effect that he or she is giving under the document, so a POA should be executed as early into the planning process as possible. The "durable" aspect of this power gives the "donee" or "agent" – the person to whom the power is given – the right to continue to handle the finances of the donor even after the donor can no longer handle his or her own affairs.

In New York, the 2010 reform of the standard POA was meant to help fight elder abuse and fraud, but a few of the requirements can invalidate a POA that is otherwise clear and direct. Each state has its own requirements for preparation and execution of a POA, so it's best to find a lawyer to prepare and supervise the execution of the document, and we always execute a few originals as many jurisdictions require filing of an original copy of the Power of Attorney with the deed and transfer documents if used in the transaction. Of course, if the parent is still mentally "with it," a POA may not be necessary, and the parent can sign the contract, deed, etc., personally.

Issues relating to money in the sale of a property are important for a simple reason – a home is the single most valuable asset most people own, and when selling it, we want the best value we can get. If you do not plan to paint or otherwise update or stage the home before it is listed for sale, the best way to minimize unexpected costs between contract and closing is to make certain that the home is being listed "AS IS" and to include provisions in the contract of sale that limit the seller's obligations to fix, repair, replace, or restore anything that is found to be broken or failing after the contract is signed.

When evaluating a buyer's offer, keep legal fees, brokers' commissions, mortgage balances, and taxes in mind. In addition to taxes due to the cities and states on the sale of a property, most long-term homeowners will have a major capital gain on sale. If, after the sale, the parent will no longer be a resident of the state where the property is sold, that state may require withholding of any capital gains taxes from the sale with any refund due only upon filing of the parent's final state tax return.

Helpful Hints

In Manhattan, it is very common for real estate agents to become experts on specific buildings and can be relied upon to get all of the information you need to handle the sale of the property.

Matt's advice clearly illustrates why you are best advised to work with a team of professionals – a real estate agent; attorney familiar with estates and local jurisdiction legal and regulatory matters; a financial advisor who can identify ways to save money on the transaction and a mortgage consultant who can help you refinance and existing mortgage or qualify a buyer.

Issues relating to the "title" to the property, the assorted rights of the buyer to the property against neighbors, government, creditors, and others, can take a number of forms referred to as "encumbrances" or "defects" in title. In the contract of sale, your parent will assure the buyer that the property described in the contract is the property the buyer will get at closing (referred to as "marketable title"). The buyer will order title insurance, and the title insurer will create a list of encumbrances that must be resolved by the seller to make the title marketable.

The most common kinds of encumbrances are mortgages and home equity loans/lines of credit, outstanding certificates of occupancy, open permits, physical areas "out of possession", bureaucratic violations, tickets, and judgments, and, in the case of a widowed seller, documentation relating to the spouse's death and his or her estate's tax and debt status. The seller's obligation to resolve encumbrances can be limited in the contract; for example, a contract can give the seller the option to cancel the contract if the cost of curing defects in title exceeds a certain dollar amount. You may decide that the cost is small compared to the purchase price, but if not, the liability is limited.

Finally, the practical considerations of selling property and closing on the sale can be mundane but important. Buyers may ask you questions about the age of appliances and roof, the status of termite treatment, the history of the property and neighbors, etc., that you may not be able to answer. Follow your common sense here: the best practice is to avoid making representations on behalf of your parent. You are best advised to rely on the advice of a real estate professional experienced with the community in general or maybe even the specific property. The buyer has the right to have the home inspected independently, and only your actual knowledge of particular conditions – lead paint, leaking fuel tanks and septic systems, asbestos, and other hazardous conditions – should be shared.

As Susan discusses later in this chapter, an upcoming closing can cause last-minute seller's remorse. As difficult as these feelings can be to overcome, a lawsuit for specific performance of the contract is worse. The importance of clear communication with your parent about why the home must be sold and when he or she will have to move cannot be understated. If you or your parent feels that the closing will be too emotional or physically exhausting, the POA discussed above becomes even more useful.

Sharpening the Pencil

Can your parent afford to make any move at all? Will financial resources determine the type of facility or living arrangement you chose? Does your parent have long-term care insurance? Can you afford to chip in not just with your time and emotional support, but also with the financial needs? What insurance resources are available to plan for future needs? Are your siblings willing to participate in the immediate physical move and/or the long term expenses? How much time over the long term are you, the principal caregiver, and/or siblings or others prepared to give to the parent? How do you deal with your own guilt and parents' unrealistic demands on your time? How will you supplement your availability with other services? How does your time and availability impact on the type of living arrangement that will be selected? Remember that under the Family Leave Act, you can take up to 12 weeks each year of unpaid leave to assist a sick family member. What are insurance and living costs now and what will they be in the new location? A review of these items will help guide you as to how to involve external advisers - clergy, lawyers, accountants, doctors, neighbors - to help you and your caregiver team gather information and make the decision. It will also reveal and address hidden costs - penalties for premature withdrawal of funds from a CD, for example, and how to avoid them.

Most people hate to talk about money. Women of my generation are especially uncomfortable - we were all taught as young girls that it was not polite to ask what something cost, what people made, how much insurance you had or what your bank balance looked like. Assuming that you are reading this book because a move for your parent is imminent, I will not scold or suggest that you should have planned ahead, but before proceeding further, it is crucial to get a firm handle on what your loved one's resources are and that additional resources you and your siblings are prepared to add to the equation.

I need to get something clear up front. Mom was tight with a buck. She avoided long-distance phone charges, she didn't waste money on things she didn't need and rarely indulged in luxuries for herself. My father used to call this "widow's syndrome" - the fear that one would outlive one's money, but for Mom, it was more a reflection of having lived through the depression.

The six years I spent after Dad died working on Mom's taxes was a big help when it came to helping her plan her move in that I understood exactly what her financial resources were. I knew how much she received in Social Security each month, knew what her stock portfolio looked like and was familiar with her bank balances. Eventually, through research using the tax assessors' records, I was able to determine the approximate value of her only other major asset - a beach house which would be sold. I also knew what her debts and financial obligations looked like. This side of the ledger is just as important in planning your move as is understanding the assets.

In my mother's case, she was debt free. If your parent would rather consult a professional than trust this information to you, or if you do not feel up to the task, or do not already have a family accountant familiar with the financial situation, call the **National Association of Personal Financial Advisors** (http://napfa.org/800-366-2732) and ask for a list of financial planners with expertise in issues facing the elderly. Some experts recommend that your parent make you a co-signer on their checking account, but one attorney I spoke with disagrees. He suggested that the better approach is a power of attorney which would give you the authority to write checks in case of emergency, physical impairment or death. The problem with co-ownership of the account is the tax liability you would face after your loved one dies when splitting up the asset with other beneficiaries. Check with your own attorney or accountant to determine the best way to handle your individual situation.

Selling the Family Home

The sale of a house can be a good source of income for a senior on a fixed income. Generally, our parents' homes are free and clear of mortgages and can be converted to cash which can be invested to produce income. Frequently, this is the most emotional part of "Moving Mom" both for your loved one and for the children, now presumably adults that may have grown up in the home or brought their own children to the beach house. Memories are built on these foundations and can be more difficult to part with than material possessions.

Mother agreed reluctantly that the house on Cape Cod which had been home for thirty summers would have to be sold. Living in Virginia and no longer driving, it would be too difficult and expensive to travel to the Cape and arrange for transportation while she was there. Dad bought the house when I was a junior in high school, so it did not represent childhood memories for me or my brother. But I had fond memories of weekends at the beach with friends and family as a young adult.

Importantly, my father had loved the house and had dedicated leisure hours over nearly thirty years to trying to get grass to grow in the sandy soil. Dad hoped the house would continue to bring the family together each summer and that his children and grandchildren would derive pleasure from this legacy that had given him so much pleasure during his lifetime. But Dad had been the caregiver to that house. Mom hated to part with the money it took to paint the shutters and trim, keep the hedges groomed and the other upkeep necessities. And her support network was 600 miles away. When a new roof was needed, Dick and I had to spend our summer vacation with Mom, during which two week period we found a reputable roofer, got estimates, hired him and supervised the work and, finally, stood over Mom while she reluctantly wrote the check to pay for the repair. The repairman's recommendation that some of the shingles on the front of the house would have to be replaced soon was met with complete avoidance.

When the decision to sell was made, Dick researched the value of property by examining what similar properties had sold for in recent months and how, in general, property in the neighborhood was selling. Mom loved the house and saw only its good qualities. She loved the large kitchen and screened porch and thought the two driveways and the three bedrooms would be attractive to any buyer. She did not see that the bedrooms were tiny, the appliances in the kitchen old or that the one bathroom was at least 20 years out of date. The condition just did not measure up to the other homes in the neighborhood that had sold for the price my Mom would have liked to have received.

Dick also interviewed real estate agents and found one who proved to be a superb professional in setting a price, finding a buyer, and smoothing out the difficulties of the sale.

And there were plenty of difficulties. The first thing we had to do was clear out Mom's belongings (and our own) because in all likelihood we would not be returning to the house. What to throw out or give away and what to keep were difficult decisions. The realtor recommended pulling up an old, soiled rug to expose the hardwood floors, a move Mom thought to be a mistake and she resisted but relented paying someone $200 to polish the floors and clean the house. A bargain to be sure! The realtor, Linda, made the arrangements and checked on the work, and she hired an electrician to make minor repairs to an outside light. Mom continued to believe, and would tell anyone who would listen, that the house was worth a great deal more than the recommended asking price. She kept talking about real estate values that had existed seven years earlier before the market crashed, and failed to accept that a fair price was what the market would offer. Linda's documentation and Dick's and my pleading got her to agree. A buyer was found within three months. When the inspection revealed that the septic field would have to be replaced at a cost of more than $2,000, the deal almost fell through. Mom didn't want to pay for it. She thought that "someone else" should pay for it. We carefully explained that the real estate agent's commission would have to be split with the agent for the purchaser and with her office and that there wasn't enough left to cover the cost of the repair. We then explained that the purchaser was not in a position to pay more than he had already bid for the property. She was prepared to let the deal fall through and see what happened the following spring. Dick had to carefully explain to her that now that the septic problem had been discovered, it would have to be repaired whether she sold the house or not and even if she raised the asking price, she would have to front the money to make the needed repairs. Dick explained what keeping the property would cost:

1. Repair to septic field
2. Costs associated with closing the house for the winter (plumber, etc.)
3. Taxes
4. Utility charges
5. Costs associated with opening the house in the spring
6. Lost interest on income from sale of property (this was in the day when our money actually did earn interest!)

When these were added up and presented in this manner, Mom reluctantly agreed, but still believed in her heart of hearts that she could have received more from the sale. I believe she was relieved, however, that she no longer had to pay the above bills that irked her every time she wrote a check.

We were lucky that we found such a resourceful real estate agent who helped do the things that today are in the realm of a good stager.

In Manhattan, we frequently rely on the expertise of Barbara Brock, Founder and President of **A Proper Place (Sold With Style)**, New York, NY who contributes the following advice:

The profession of Home Staging is a relatively new field in selling real estate. Our role as stagers is to help sellers (and brokers) with the preparation and presentation of their real estate before it is put on the market. Often the preparation is not only about attacking the condition of the physical space, but also about the psychology of the seller leaving the property.

One of the biggest by products of hiring a staging professional is that our presence helps the seller to break the attachment to the home. We not only outline what needs to be done, but we are there to facilitate what needs to be done. This can be a huge responsibility lifted from the heirs of an estate or from a seller's shoulders. Stagers can refer or oversee

1) organizers,
2) movers,
3) estate sellers,

4) auction houses, and

5) contractors to facilitate the pre-sale.

Barbara Corcoran, a noted NBC Real Estate commentator, recently noted, "Hiring a stager can actually save you money. The cost might be less than you think."

After this decision has been made to sell, the staging profession emphasizes that the goal of putting your house on the market is to attract a Buyer.

To begin with, a consultation from a staging professional will give all parties a blue print of what needs to be done, how to go about readying the property for sale and how it needs to be presented or "staged" at the Open House. As a stager tours the property, notes will be taken on the "condition and the presentation" of the property. The stager sees the property through the eyes of a buyer and puts together a "wish list" of how the property can be transformed which is then discussed with the seller and broker. A plan is put together in terms of budget, priority and dividing up responsibility of getting things done.

I often recommend that a photograph (or video) be taken to remember, "the way it was." This serves two purposes – memory and insurance purposes. A wide-angle camera is preferred for taking exterior and interior room shots, but if one is not available, a regular 35 mm camera will be fine. Take the front and back of the home and the most important rooms – living room, dining room, kitchen, master bedroom and any other room that is a favorite. Before taking a photograph, a room needs to be clean, neatened, beds made, counters and tabletops clear of clutter. You don't want to remember the clutter and a camera picks up minutia.

I also recommend taking a photograph of individual items. Before my mother passed away, I photographed 465 items of furnishings and accessories. I then put these in a master list with a check box beside each photo, distributed this list to my 6 brothers and sisters with the request that they initial what their choices were. We were able to decide ahead of time who wanted what on the most important pieces, thereby avoiding hard feelings at the time of death. This also enables the elder person to be in on the conversation and to know that some of their possessions will live on.

In a nutshell, there are 5 steps to readying a furnished occupied or estate home:

1. Edit and sort your furnishings. Use this time to decide on what you want to keep and what you want to donate, give away, or sell. We recommend packing all out of season clothes, and sundries. For the selling season, get lean and mean.
2. Move or store 50% of the furniture in the home. You will be moving anyway, so pack up early. Buyers cannot see the space if there is too much furniture, clutter or highly decorated spaces. Your style is YOUR STYLE. Buyers are concerned with where they can eat, sleep and entertain. Therefore the main rooms are the living room, dining room and master bedroom.
3. Make repairs to the home. Buyer's do not want to purchase your "to do" list. The more you make this "buyer ready", the faster your home will sell. *
4. Deep clean the home — closets, shelves, floors, kitchen appliances, bathroom fixtures, windows, yards, garages. You can feel when a home is dirty and odors are ghastly if they are prominent.
5. Arrange the home attractively. Key points are furniture placement, lighting, art work, well placed accessories, fresh linens in the bathroom and bedroom.**

* There is an OLD conversation that a buyer will want to remodel kitchens and bathrooms the way they want to. Today, people will pay more and buy faster if kitchens and bathrooms are updated. They will still remodel, but they can take their time about doing so.

** I recommend one set of bed and bath linens be set aside strictly for open houses. Other times, these can be stored on a shelf or basket.

Other Assets

Thank you Barbara for that great advice!

We went through the same cash analysis in the sale of Mom's car as we did with the house. Insurance savings alone were nearly $2,000 per year, with maintenance, depreciation and gas and oil adding another $2,000. This was one area; however, where Mom never minded spending money.

Her car was closely associated with her independence and she never got over giving it up and not driving anymore.

Other sources of income include the cash value of life insurance, sale of other assets, and reduction of expenses. Long-term care insurance is available but expensive and requires advance planning - it should be purchased before age 65. Protecting assets from Medicare is another aspect of long-term financial planning. This can be accomplished through the transfer of assets to beneficiaries, but such a transfer must be accomplished 36 months in advance of a claim. Irrevocable living trusts must be set up five years before a Medicare claim. You can also claim your parent as a dependent under certain circumstances and make a loan for current expenses against his/her estate.

For all of the above, it is important to work with a professional estate planner who knows current tax law and will keep you informed of changes in the tax code.

Take Action: Complete a Financial Worksheet

Assets

Cash

Checking Accounts	$
Savings Accounts	$
Certificates of deposit	$
Money market accounts	$
Money-market funds	$
Treasury bills	$

Retirement funds

IRAs	$
401(ks), 403(bs)	$
Annuities	$
Deferred compensation	$

Investments

Life insurance (cash value)	$
Bonds	$
Stocks	$
Mutual funds	$
Real estate	$

Tangible Assets

Home(s)	$
Car(s)	$
Other	$
TOTAL ASSETS	$

LIABILITIES

Credit card balances	$
Personal loans	$
Mortgage(s)	$
Business loans	$
TOTAL LIABILITIES	$

MONTHLY INCOME

Social Security	$
Spouse's pension	$
Your pension	$
Dividends	$
Other	$

TOTAL MONTHLY INCOME $

Other Resources:

- **Aging Network Services**, http://agingnets.com
- **Leading Age** http://www.leadingage.org/LeadingAge's Consumer Hub offers information and support to help people make the most of the aging experience. This includes a directory of not-for-profit organizations committed to meeting people's needs and preferences as they age.
- **AARP.org** (search caregiver) has a wealth of information on caregiver issues and resources.

Helpful Hints

Help is just a click away...
Experience Registry, **National Academy of Elder Law Attorneys**, http://www.naela.org/public
520- 881-4005
1604 North Country Club Road, Tucson, Arizona 85716.
The National Academy of Elder Law Attorneys will not provide a referral, but you can purchase its directory of 2,600 members nationwide. According to its own literature, NAELA "...is a professional association of attorneys concerned with improving the availability of legal services to older persons."

Chapter Six

Finding the Right Solution

I can't say enough good things about well-run assisted living communities. Mom chose the Jefferson, a Marriott Senior Residence in Northern Virginia. The minimum age to purchase one of the beautiful apartments is 55 and some residents had already actively celebrated their 100th birthdays when we discovered this great alternative. Mom's apartment was a one bedroom that was carefully designed to meet the needs of the elderly. The kitchen was similar to many that are typical here in New York where many people do a limited amount of cooking. At the Jefferson in Arlington, VA and other similar senior resident communities, residents eat at least one meal, generally dinner, in the common dining room. The kitchen had a small dishwasher, refrigerator and stove. The cabinet space was sufficient to meet the pared down inventory of dishes, pots and pans.

Once my father died, Mom stopped cooking and began relying on frozen dinners and other prepared foods. For a diabetic with a heart condition, the results were disastrous. Mom's general health declined and her diabetes worsened. The hot meal she received every night at the Jefferson provided a better nutritional balance than before the move.

When I was growing up, my mother was an immaculate house keeper. Again, however, as time passed, her loss of energy and motivation combined put an end to cleaning habits of a lifetime. My husband and I hated to visit her apartment in Boston or the house on Cape Cod because the dust was so bad in the spare room where we stayed. At the Jefferson, Mom's monthly fee included the services of a housekeeper once a week who dusted, cleaned the bathroom and changed and washed the linens.

Each apartment is equipped with an emergency button used to call for assistance. In addition, two portable units are given to each resident to either be hung around the neck, placed beside the tub or bed or wherever the person is in the apartment. This proved a life-saver when Mom broke her hip in the bathroom.

The brightly lit hallways are equally well-planned. Wide enough to accommodate wheelchairs or emergency equipment, what appears to be a chair rail in each hallway is actually a handgrip, recessed from the wall.

A complete program of education, sports, and cultural activities is also available at this and other similar properties. After a case of pneumonia and a minor heart attack, my mother, at the suggestion of her cardiologist, began participating in an aerobics program - the first organized sports activity of her life. Tickets to ball games, rides to movie theaters and malls, special seating at the Kennedy Center for Performing Arts awere just a few of monthly list of activities available to the active seniors who reside at the Jefferson. And of course there are card groups - canasta, bridge and Mom's favorite - poker, which she usually played twice a week.

More mundane but necessary services are also provided. Three times each week transportation is provided to nearby grocery stores. Transportation to doctor's visits is provided two days per week.

Future planning for deteriorating health - both temporary and permanent - is an important part of the concept of most independent and assisted living facilities. At the Jefferson, a nurse is on site 24-hours per day and a doctor on call. Two entire floors in one wing are turned over to nursing care (at additional cost). RNs and LPNs and nurses' aides are available for hourly work for residents at reasonable rates. For example, if a resident were temporarily incapacitated, they could hire a nurse's aide to visit in their own apartment to help dress and bathe or to administer medication.

Take Action: Visit Several Assisted and Independent Living Facilities

Create an Assisted Living and Condominium Checklist.

Include:

- **Location:**
  - distance from your home
  - distance from your office
  - distance from hospital
  - access to shopping
  - access to public transportation

- **Availability:**
  - units currently available
  - under construction - delivery date:
  - waiting list
  - average wait:
  - size options
  - price options
  - how many units are sold? available?
  - is the development free of liens?
  - has developer built similar properties?

- **Costs:**
  - purchase price
  - is parking included?
    - self-parking
    - valet
  - does condo unit become part of owner's estate or
  - does condo developer maintain rights after death of owner?
  - condo fee?
  - other fees?
  - tax rate
  - financing options

- **Services:**
  - transportation:
  - shopping

- library
- doctor's visits
- cultural/social activities
- religious services

- **Medical**
  - Doctor on premises
  - Doctor on call
  - Nurse on premises
  - Nurse on call

- **Food**
  - meal plans (B, L, D)
  - cost
  - guests welcome
  - limitations
  - cost

- **Housekeeping**
  - frequency
  - cost

- **Social activities:**
  - check both availability and cost.
  - staff or volunteer planning?
  - cards
  - movies
  - cultural events
  - aerobics
  - theme parties
  - golf
  - swimming
  - tennis
  - exercise room
  - trips
  - religious services
  - scheduled visits by clergy

- **Rehabilitative services**
  - On-site nursing home
  - On-site Alzheimer's care

- **Security**
  - restricted access to lobbies
  - restricted access to elevators
  - restricted access to parking
  - reception desk staffed what hours?
  - guard(s) on duty 24 hours
  - Access for wheelchairs,
  - walkers

- **General ambience**
  - decorations
  - upkeep
  - fresh flowers indoors
  - landscaping

Chapter Seven

Moving Mom

The decision to move has been made and the new home has been selected. Whether to your home, a new condominium or an assisted living rental unit, the physical demands of cleaning out and closing down the old home (or homes) and moving into the new cannot be avoided. As the caregiver, you must facilitate the actual physical move. If you approach the task from a project management viewpoint, the move will go more smoothly. Advance planning, physical as well as "intellectual" work is necessary at Mom's existing residence and in the new locale as well. This chapter will deal with the advance planning at the "move out" home.

The Project Manager

The first step is to determine who will be ultimately responsible for decision making, there can only be one team captain, but, you can and should make assignments.

A great deal of patience is required during this period and the more leeway your parent will give you to make decisions - which mover to hire, what furniture will be given away or sold, when and where the garage sale will be held - the easier it will be for you. But involving your parent in these decisions can be used to help show them that they are still in control over their own lives and can make decisions for themselves.

After it has been decided that you will be the "project manager" for the move, establish a time schedule for visits to accomplish the various tasks. Don't try to make all decisions at one time and don't try to clean out a lifetime of possessions in one visit. For Mom's move, she picked out her new condominium during a January visit, placed a deposit in February, and moved in July 1. I appreciated the time available to clear the clutter, make trips to Hadassah and Goodwill with donated items and decide what would be packed and moved. Cindy Myer of Ridgewood Moving Services is fond of saying "Don't trash your move by moving your trash." Block out time on your calendar when you can spend a few days at a time to handle the various activities you will be overseeing. I scheduled one visit during tax-time so that I could prepare Mom's returns at the same time I was working on cleaning out the basement.

Down Sizing

A frequently delicate and time consuming task is working with the parent in preparing the home for the move. Be prepared for difficulty in getting your parent to determine what will be given away to friends and family, donated to charity or sold. This can be one of the toughest parts of the move and is a source of humor, poignancy and just plain hard work. In most cases the new living arrangement will be smaller than the one from which the parent is moving. My sister-in-law Peggy's mother had a wonderful answer to the problem of what to do with many of her possessions as she prepared to move from her home - she gave everything which had been a gift back to the person who had given it to her. She was able to say, "I have received many years of pleasure from this vase. I kept it in my living room where I could look at it every day. Now that I am moving into smaller quarters, I would like you to be able to get back some of the enjoyment you provided me with this gift."

Giving up possessions is frequently a symbolic and painful experience for an older person. Many feel that it represents the end of a chapter in their lives. My mother, for example, could not part with her twelve complete place settings of "good" china. Even though she knew in her heart that her cooking and entertaining days were over, she was not ready to part with even one place setting. She finally parted with the set as a wedding gift to a favorite grandchild knowing she would enjoy dining on her prized china at Thanksgiving.

Dick and I have been downsizing gradually over the past decade and every time we move to a new location or smaller quarters, I can't believe how liberating it has become to donate or gift the many items that I once thought I could not live without. At some point in time, your material goods possess you rather than you them and limit your options on how much space you need and where you can live.

Moving the Medical History

Among the other tasks to complete, and a very important one, is meeting with or talking to doctors to arrange transitional medications, and recommendations or referrals for medical care in the new location. It is also important to arrange for the transfer of medical records and prescriptions. To prepare for the transition to new doctors, I suggested to Mom that she ask each of her physicians to provide her with prescriptions for three months of each of her medications, rather than the one month they had been giving her. I didn't know at the time, and no one told me, that the reason that the prescriptions were issued one month at a time is that was all typical insurance companies will cover. When I went to the pharmacy to pick up the prescriptions, the pharmacist informed me that BC/BS would not pay for a 90 day supply. I tried explaining the circumstances - Mom was moving to a new area, she was dependent upon her medications and that it might take more than 30 days in her new location to get to see new doctors who would issue new medications. As the pharmacy that filled her prescriptions was a national chain with stores in Mom's new location, I had hoped that they would be able to forward her prescription records. I was told that they could not transfer prescriptions out of state. BC/BS had already agreed that they would cover her insurance for two additional months in the new location until she could make arrangements to transfer her policy to a local provider. I spent more than 20 hours at the pharmacy and later on the phone with the pharmacy, Blue Cross Blue Shield and the managed care agency before the problem was solved. The process was frustrating. Every time I thought I had it straightened out, something new would happen. I got "approval codes" directly from BC/BS (an exception to their policy), but the computer at the pharmacy wouldn't accept the codes. It took more than a month before the problem was finally straightened out. Be prepared. You should consult your insurance provider about ordering 90-day prescriptions from online providers.

Whether you fill the prescriptions before or after the move, it is a good idea to have and keep a list of all of the medications he/she is taking. New doctors will want to see what has been prescribed and in an emergency this is an important time (and maybe even life) saver.

Make certain you include on your list the medication, dosage, prescribing doctor (and phone number) as well as the fulfilling pharmacy information.

During your visits include closing out checking and bank accounts, credit card accounts for local establishments, and address changes for accounts and mail that will be forwarded to the new location. Create a checklist to make certain each account has been taken care of. Keep track of the names of people you speak with on the phone and dates of contact.

> **Take Action**
> ───────────
> 1. Schedule enough time to transfer prescription medications.
> 2. Check with the pharmacist on procedures and insurance requirements.
> 3. Make a list of all prescriptions.

Likewise, a discussion in person or on the phone with an attorney regarding wills and powers of attorney should be accomplished at this point.

Before contacting potential moving companies, inventory all items in the home, including clothing and fine art. A physical inventory is time consuming but will help you to decide what will be moved, sold or donated. With a copy of the inventory in hand, you can discuss the pros and cons of the disposition of each item. The value of each item to be donated will be used when you contact the volunteer agency that will receive your donations and can be used later in preparing tax returns. The inventory will also be your first draft list for the tag sale, although I recommend you transfer the items to a separate "tag sale inventory" prior to the sale.

This can also be used if you plan to sell items on craigslist or e-bay. From my personal experience, I would never hold another tag sale nor would I advertise. The negotiations add an additional level of stress and many people, myself included, do not want strangers in our homes. In Manhattan, it would be difficult to hold a tag sale and many buildings would not allow it. Alternatively, donation to a reputable charity is relatively easy and provides good documentation for tax preparation. For many charities, you will have to provide the list of items to be donated and you establish the value. They merely provide documentation that they picked the item up. Barbara's suggestion that you take photographs of each item is an important part of this process.

After the tag sale, double check your list and do a final inventory of all items in the home which will be moved to the new location. It is important that this be completed before contacting movers. The cost of a long distance move is determined by the weight of the load, and movers are expert at determining the approximate weight of a load based on the items to be moved. You will save their time and your own if you have a complete, room-by-room inventory before calling for an estimate. Some movers will give you an estimate over the phone based on your faxed or mailed inventory list but most movers will want to see the house, what obstacles exist to removing furniture, location of stairs, even the size of the street.

> ### Helpful Hint
> Ask the moving company if they supply free "used" boxes, many companies recycle. There are local moving companies that are agents for national vanlines. For example Ridgewood is an agent for Arpin Van lines enabling it to provide assistance for relocations all over the world.

Selecting a Mover

According to Cindy Myer, CEO of Ridgewood Moving Services, a referral from a friend or colleague is of course the best way to start your selection process. Someone in the industry such as a Realtor, Real Estate

Attorney, Mortgage broker, etc. should have referrals on hand as well. Once you receive several names you may check with the Better Business Bureau and the local movers' assocation in your state for their status and reputation. In the state of New Jersey where Ridgewood Moving is located the associaton is NJWMA (NJ Warehousemen and Movers Assocation). You can view a list of Moving Companies within your geographic area and select a company from that list. You can also see which Movers are members of *Circle of Excellence*, an elite group that needs to meet certain criteria. Another vehicle for selecting a moving company is the National Movers Association also know as AMSA. They have a promover program and are the "watch dogs" for the nation.

Your Mover should have a license and be fully insured. You may want to view their website and find out how long they have been in business. A reputable mover will also be willing to provide you with referrals to past customers.

A Moving Consultant should provide you with a visual survey in an effort to discuss your needs and take an inventory of the belongings being moved. At the end of the visit you should be provided with or sent that list. For out of state moves a tractor trailer would be used for moving the distance. The Moving Consultant should be checking the origin to make sure that the trailer can fit on the local streets. If you are moving out of a city then a "shuttle" would be required, which is normally the agent's 24 foot box truck needed to deliver the items to the larger vehicle. Again, this all should have been determined up front for there are additional charges for this service. The same is true on destination.

Helpful Hints

Owners cannot turn off their metered services until the date of closing. At that time, they need to be taken out of your name and the new owners need to have services transferred into their names.

Request final meter readings and final bills.

Tenants need to notify utilities that as of a certain date (either move out date or lease termination date) that the utilities are no longer to be in your name.

Some moving companies have special services and packages for seniors. Arpin has a special package providing free materials, set ups and discounted valuation protection. Our company provides a special hand held program for our *Very Special Senior*. We leave behind a "file folder" complete with Smooth Move Tips and guideline to assist during the weeks leading up to the move. This file is also used for our VIP Seniors to capture important papers in one spot. We also try to be a resource for our clients for items that they may need to dispose of or want to donate. Our donation resource list is on our website.

Also, keep in mind the busiest time of year is June through August. If possible try to plan your move during off season months and even better is mid month and mid week. You should get better crews and better prices if you can plan accordingly.

We didn't know it at the time, but everything Cindy talks about concerning street size and shuttles was an important consideration in our move, but we were not prepared. We selected a well-known national mover after a visit from their sales representative. The sales rep came to the house, and went room by room with a computerized form determining what would be moved and what wouldn't. As we hadn't decided on certain items, the estimate was just that - an estimate subject to changes Mom would make as to what would be taken away. The decision to move an old and heavy piece of furniture, or boxes of books that have no special value, are made a lot easier when you understand how much per pound it will cost to bring them to the new location. I interviewed five movers over the telephone and three in person. I discovered as Cindy said that unless you had enough possessions for an entire van, your household goods would be placed on a van with one or two other households. Even movers you think are independents and you believe will handle your move from start to finish, don't. They may use their own people to pack your goods and move them onto their truck. From that point on, however, they are off-loaded

Helpful Hints

Notify your providers of your upcoming move
- Telephone
- Cell phone
- Cable TV
- Electric/Gas/
- Water Company
- Misc; landscapers, exterminators, alarm, etc.

onto another van which will make the interstate trip and are off-loaded by that company's local contractor. So, instead of dealing with one company, you are really dealing with three. I selected a large, nationally known company because I assumed that they would have the most consistent service in loading Mom, moving her goods from Massachusetts to Virginia and unloading her. I was wrong - but more of that later.

After all my advance planning, I was surprised when on moving day, a sinewy moving man showed up at our door, sans moving truck, to say that he didn't think the van would make it down the street. Furthermore, he asked, why were there cars parked in front of our house and our neighbors'. "Didn't anyone tell you that the street would have to be cleared so we could park the van?", he asked. Well, no. Nobody told us. The next piece of news was that he would have to find out if the local mover could provide a "transfer" truck. This meant that the movers would put Mom's furniture on a truck in front of our house, drive three blocks to the van, unload the furniture and reload it on the van. Three moves instead of one. Three chances for furniture and possessions to be damaged or lost. We stood around for a couple of hours not knowing what was happening. Finally, in the early afternoon we were notified that the move would have to be delayed until the next day.

> **Take Action**
>
> - Photograph possessions to be sold, donated or moved.
> - Create an inventory.
> - Interview Moving Companies and get bids.
> - Select a mover.

There we stood - every last box packed and sealed tight, the electric company notified, the mattresses stripped and covered with plastic, the refrigerator emptied and phone service to be terminated that afternoon. Our original plan was that after the movers left, we would drive to Cape Cod to close up that house and take away any last items that we wanted to keep after the house was sold. Mom really wanted to stay. She wanted to personally watch and supervise as each last piece left the house. But we finally convinced her that was not reasonable. My sister-in-law Peggy took Mom in her car to the Cape to begin the process of closing the house and I stayed, sleeping on the plastic-wrapped sofa, to supervise the next day's move.

Take Action: Create an Inventory for the Move and the Tag Sale

Use your own form or request one from a moving company. Ridgewood's web site, http://ridgewoodmoving.com/video9.html, has great videos to help you through all stages of the preparation. Don't forget to include the garage if there is one, or possible off-site storage areas.

Helpful Hints

Typical Box Usage:

Small Box:	Books, records, canned goods
Medium:	Pots, pans, lines, etc.
Large:	Blankets, pillows, bulky items
XLarge:	Toys, baskets, lighter bulky items, lamp shades
Wardrobe:	2 ft closet hanging clothes, shoes
Picture/Mirror:	Glass, pictures, mirrors
Dishpack:	China, lamps, all fragile items

Crating:

Special constructed crates are built to protect special items:

Antiques, mirrors, glass/marble table tops, art work, chandeliers, statues

---

Take Action: Compile a List of Important Resources

Be certain to keep a special list that contains contact information for your mover, the realtors on the sell and purchase side, closing attorneys and more. Create your own list and include the names and contact information for:

- Mover
- Realtor (sale)
- Realtor (purchase)
- Assisted Living Facility Administrator
- Closing attorney (sale)
- Closing attorney (purchase)
- Goodwill Industries/ Salvation Army
- Veterans Group
- Bank Manger (old)
- Bank Manager (new)

Take Action

Moving Week Count down:
- ✓ Plan meals that will use us your food
- ✓ Have your car serviced if you are traveling
- ✓ Dispose of common household items
- ✓ Return library books and video rentals
- ✓ Collect items that are being cleaned
- ✓ Find appliance manuals for the new owner/occupant that are staying
- ✓ Pack an overnight bag/toiletries
- ✓ Set aside valuable and important papers such as; insurance policies, pet documents, home purchase/ sale documents, mortgage documents, wills, financial records, stock certificates, social security cards, passports, birth certificates, medical records, prescriptions, bank records, check books.

Thanks to Ridgewood Moving and CEO Cindy Meyer for the helpful hints and action items in this chapter.

Chapter Eight

Getting Ready
in the New Home

It's not all about the home your loved one is vacating. Advance work is also needed at the "receiving" end. It is important that thought be given to readying the new home, be it your own home or a nursing home, for Mom's arrival. Review the lists you compiled from the information in the preceding chapter, and make certain your check list includes identifying medical providers in the appropriate specialties who are geographically convenient, opening new bank accounts, reserving a safety deposit box, establishing new prescription drug accounts, transferring and/or acquiring medical and personal property insurance, and transferring Social Security and other pension or annuity deposits. *Don't forget to register Mom to vote!* It is also a good idea to revalidate wills and powers of attorney in accordance with the laws in the new location if an interstate move has been made. If the parent is still driving a car it will be necessary to arrange for a test for a new driver's license. The specific tasks required will vary by living arrangement choice, but generally include: arranging for phone service and other installation requirements, making repairs or installing window treatments, and doing a floor plan of new home to make certain furniture and possessions will fit. It is also a good idea to have any repairs or upgrades completed before the scheduled move. If appropriate, rent an off-site storage bin to handle all those things Mom couldn't quite part with yet and won't fit in the new living arrangement. We did that for my mother and it gave my nieces and nephews a convenient place to take a look at things and decide which items they would like for themselves. If moving into a nursing home, apartment or condominium it is necessary to schedule the move-in and reserve elevators and find out what insurance the mover must provide to the building or deposits or fees you must pay prior to the move date.

Judy put special love and consideration into making her mother's new house a welcoming and familiar home. "I incorporated her old life with a brand new life. I took little pictures, and some of the furniture, precious things that she really loved no matter how they looked, and then I bought new things. When she showed up for the first day and saw it, she was so taken with the look of the place that the fear that she had that she was going to be giving up everything that was important to her just wasn't there. It's just like my store - it's so funny. I gave her a piece of the old with the new."

After a struggle to get her to part with an old, uncomfortable and damaged sofa bed, my Mom enjoyed shopping for a new couch for the living room, purchased fabric for a matching swag over the windows and coordinated with fabric to reupholster the seats on her dining room chairs. The new apartment was an adventure in decorating that helped Mom to look forward and to realize that, even at her age; she could enjoy "new" things. She was very proud of her home and loved to have visits from family and friends so she could show it off. For us, this was an important counterbalance to the concerns about "giving up" some of the old possessions and down-sizing one's life

Take Action: Create a Check List for pre-move activities in new location.

> ## Take Action
>
> **Check List**
> - Measure all rooms for furniture placement
> - Measure all windows for shades, etc.
> - Open bank account
>   - Mail signature cards to Mom with return envelope
>   - Ask bank to file change of Social Security deposit
>   - Secure Safety Deposit Box for important papers
> - Check on move-in procedures at the new location
> - Secure move-in date
> - Arrange, where needed, for advance cleaning crew
> - Arrange for delivery of newly purchased furniture, appliances
> - Get recommendations for physicians
> - Establish account at local pharmacy

Chapter Nine

The Move

We are down to the wire and the move is at hand. This chapter will provide hints on how to have a smooth move and what to do when, despite your efforts, it isn't smooth. From the practical tasks such as shutting off utilities to the trauma of saying goodbye to friends of a lifetime, the chapter will prepare the caregiver for the psychological impact both for him/herself and the parent. These can be exacerbated by your own probable exhaustion, frustration and depression.

Take Action: Create a Check List for what to do the week of the move, the day of the move.

Check List

One month before the move:

- Make a list of all possessions which will not be moved
- Hold tag sale
- Make appointment for removal of donated furniture
- Reconfirm moving date and move-in date with moving company
- If moving out of state/locality:
  - notify all doctors of move
  - get referrals, if appropriate, to new doctors
  - determine procedure for transfer of medical records
- Open a bank account in new community
- Have bank file form for transfer of social security direct deposit to new account
- Notify Social Security of change of address
- Notify other pension providers of change of address
- Request and complete new direct deposit forms

One Week before the move:

- Reconfirm packing date with mover
- Refill all prescription medications
- Call electric company (and other utilities) to cancel service or/transfer billing
- Take last minute unwanted clothing/furniture to charity
- Visit Post Office or visit usps.gov and file address change
- Send address change cards
- Reconfirm move in date with condo/assisted living facility

If moving to new city/state:

- Close out local bank accounts

Day before the move:

- Pack a suitcase of personal belongings for transition period
  - clothing for interim period
  - several pairs of comfortable shoes
  - medicines
  - valuables
  - important papers needed before move-in
  - telephone and address book

Chapter Ten

Moving In

A successful transition to a new life takes planning, monitoring and sensitivity to your own needs and feelings as well as those of the parent. It is important to involve an extended "team" to make move-in as easy as possible. Spending time acclimating parent to the new environment is important, but equally important to long term success can be knowing when to let go and let the parent develop a life of their own. The extent will, of course depend on the physical status of the parent and several scenarios will be addressed. Helping unpack and making the new location "home" are the obvious tasks at hands but problems and actions will vary by life style choice. If in your own home, for example, establishing rules and relationships should be done up front. Depending on the living arrangement, devise a schedule among the caregivers for checking in and checking up with the parent. Identifying community programs for seniors can help the parent to establish a network of new friends and activities that will occupy their time, increase their mental well-being and ease the burden on the caregiver. You can utilize the resources of the senior living community to ease the transition at this point. Familiarizing your

> ### *Helpful Hints*
>
> Schedule of activities in months 1-3 in new location
> - Visit new doctors
> - Establish pharmacy account
> - Visit local grocery stores

parent with resources of new community can be accomplished in many ways and is important to their sense of control over their new life.

Nursing Homes/Hospice Care

Sometimes the move is not to a new independent apartment or home. At some point a nursing home or hospice is the logical choice.

Betty learned the hard way that there are differences in nursing homes. She had been very happy with services and staff of the assisted living facility into which both her parents had moved. So when her father's condition required that he be placed in a nursing home, she chose the course of least resistance and placed him in the nursing home that was affiliated with and located near the assisted living facility. She found the staff to be neglectful and filed a complaint with the state licensing board after her father's death. Her Dad had been in declining health which was worsened by the effects of a fall at the nursing home which left him with three broken fingers. To make matters worse, a staph infection developed in those fingers. Betty came to the nursing home at 5:00 p.m. on the day her father was to have visited the orthopedic surgeon at noon. "When I got to his room it was empty. The bed was made up and neat and there was no sign of Dad." Betty's heart was in her throat as she asked the nurse where her father was. The floor nurse did not know. Betty questioned several other staff, including the Administrator of the facility and it was only after a call to the doctor's office that Betty discovered that her father had been admitted to the emergency room of the hospital and that the doctors at that moment were deciding whether or not to amputate his infected fingers.

For some families, one solution is not enough; nor is it necessarily forever. Lorna's parents, in their mid-80's, were both aging at home together in their Brooklyn apartment. Lorna was living in Riverdale with her husband and young son. Her brother and his partner were living in Philadelphia. Her Dad's illness came at a time when her Mom was struggling with vision loss in one eye and also having trouble maintaining her balance while walking on the street. They were isolated in Brooklyn with no family members nearby and Lorna very tied up with her own family and a full time job in real estate. The family needed to get some critical care for Dad as he was suffering with bladder cancer and their mother could not care for him alone. Fulltime home health care was not really an option. Their attorney suggested that they had three choices: First was to move Dad into a nursing home and get an aide to stay with Mom. Second, would be to move Dad to the Hebrew Home Nursing Home and move Mom into the adjacent independent senior living center known as River Walk. Third was to use the money they had to buy them an apartment in Riverdale and have Mom live there while Dad remained at the Hebrew Home Nursing Home until he recovered. Lorna's brother convinced Mom to go with the second option - senior living -as it would ease his mind about who was looking after her. It was pricey and she didn't relish the thought of spending all that money, but it seemed like the only really good option at the time. While River Walk is not an assisted living residence, they gave her the emotional support she needed while visiting her husband at the Home which was across the quad from her apartment. Their kindness and concern seemed to make up for the fact that what she got for $4,500 per month was basically a small one bedroom apartment with Modified American Plan of two meals a day. All of the ladies would pack up some food from the lavish breakfast and save those nice bagel sandwiches for an afternoon snack. Also included in the rent was weekly maid service and daily turndown service. Lorna's Mom stayed happily at River Walk for nearly a year and eventually Lorna's Dad passed away. She was happy at River Walk for a few months and then began to talk about the possibility of leaving for a place more in the heart of civilization with young babies, families and not the constant sight and sound of ambulances and funeral cars. The family understood her point. She was also realistically concerned about using up all of her savings. She probably had enough money left to last a few more years and then what? Also, Lorna and her brother were worried about what would happen if the blindness she had in one eye spread to the other eye. She wouldn't be able to stay alone at River Walk and the Hebrew Home had no facility for the blind. The cost of staying at River Walk and employing a full time aide was beyond their resources. In fact, their fears were realized when at one point during her year alone at River Walk she suddenly went blind in the other eye. The head of administration told Lorna she would need to get an aide to stay with her or she would have to move her mother to a facility that catered to the blind.

Then a miracle happened. The doctor was able to return some vision in her good eye. The question of "What next?" still loomed. Mom, a real trooper, who did not want to be a burden to her family, continued to worry about what would happen when her money ran out. The answer to that question received from River Walk administration did not make the family happy. They would be happy to transfer Mom into the Nursing Home. "Well, what if she is not sick at that point", Lorna asked. The answer was the expected but disappointing that was the only option.

Buying is also an Option

Thinking back to the initial attorney recommendation, Lorna's family considered buying an apartment for their Mother. This time, it would not be in Riverdale, but in Manhattan, which had always been her dream. It was also where Lorna spent her days working and where her son was enrolled in school.

Lorna's Mom is probably the only person to leave the River Walk senior residence on her own two feet into a brand new co-op apartment in the heart of the Upper West Side. Lorna's brother had to dip into his retirement savings to help with the deposit and they both worked to shore up her financial picture in order to make her acceptable to the coop's board. They pulled together as a family this time and made it happen. Lorna is pleased to report that her adjustment has been amazing. Gone are the fancy meals in the dining room, she now waits for her daily Meals On Wheels delivery which the family supplements with frozen dinners and prepared meals. She has a social worker and a wonderful safety net that came to her from the intervention of a nearby social service agency that caters to the needs of many elderly neighborhood residents. Their attention to her is greatly appreciated. She has regular visits from women who come to play Scrabble and other families who come on the holidays with baskets of goodies and homemade cards. She has also made some friends in the building, one of whom has become a close friend of Lorna's and can be counted upon in an emergency. The family is hopeful that she can stay in that apartment for a long time.

Task List – Develop a list of questions to ask at the nursing home or hospice

Sample Questions:

- Is parent eligible for Medicaid?
- What is the daily rate?
- What is the monthly rate?
- Are doctor's charges included in the fee charged?
- Are medications included in the fee?
  - If not, can you bring in your own medications to be administered at the facility (frequently purchased cheaper at your local pharmacy or through the AARP).
- If special feeding arrangements are necessary, will extra charges be incurred?
- Are wheelchairs and walkers provided?
- Is the home licensed by the state?
- Does it have any other licenses or certifications?
- Is the location convenient to your home and place of business?
- What is the ambience of the home? Are there institutional smells present in the hallways and bedrooms. Are the rooms bright and pleasant?
- Does the facility have recreational facilities and programs? Is there outdoor space which can accommodate a resident reading or sunning?
- Are residents dressed or kept in nightwear?
- Is the food prepared and presented in a healthy and appetizing manner?
- What is the medical staff?
- Other considerations relating to hobbies and interests of your particular situation

References:

www.APlaceforMom.com -The Nation's Largest FREE Elder Care Referral Service
Over 17,000 national partners
More than 300 advisors around the country

The Alzheimer's Association

www.alz.org

Local support groups, helplines, pamphlets, newsletter, referrals

The National Alliance for Caregiving:

http://www.caregiving.org/ - national resource center, information on conferences, books and training for family and professional caregivers.

The National Association of Professional Geriatric Care Managers:

www.caremanager.org

Directory of care managers who specialize in assessing your parents' financial, legal and medical needs.

Chapter Eleven

You are Not Quite Done

It isn't over when the move has been successfully completed. Things keep popping up and you will find that ongoing support will be needed both in terms of personal time and financial cost. After four years of being Mom's primary caregiver, I felt I had lost most of my friends. Rather than sharing a manicure with Monica on Saturday, I was doing Mom's grocery shopping. A movie – well, Dick would hoist the wheel chair into the car and off we would go. You will also have to continue to monitor both the psychological and physical health of your parent and yourself. It is a good idea to develop a relationship with doctors and have "Mom's" permission to discuss with them your observations of changes in behavior or mobility. A Medical Power of Attorney is a must. Budgeting your time and integrating another's frequently considerable needs into your already busy life can be a challenge.

Lori Sokol, Ph.D. and publisher of Work Life Matters and NY Residential magazines offers the following.

When you consider that fifty-nine percent of informal caregivers have jobs in addition to caring for another person, a lot of additional stress and strain are involved with caregiving. Some of the stressors a caregiver may feel include:

- Frustration and anger taking care of someone with dementia who often wanders away or becomes easily upset
- Guilt because you think that you should be able to provide better care, despite all the other things that you have to do

- Loneliness because all of the time you spend caregiving has hurt your social life
- Exhaustion when you go to bed at night

Can caregiver stress affect my health?

According to the Office on Women's Health*, although most caregivers are in good health, it is not uncommon for caregivers to have serious health problems. Research shows that caregivers:

- Are more likely to be have symptoms of depression or anxiety
- Are more likely to have a long-term medical problem, such as heart disease, cancer, diabetes, or arthritis
- Have higher levels of stress hormones
- Spend more days sick with an infectious disease
- Have a weaker immune response to the influenza, or flu, vaccine
- Have slower wound healing
- Have higher levels of obesity
- May be at higher risk for mental decline, including problems with memory and paying attention

Part of the reason that caregivers often have health problems is that they are less likely to take good care of themselves. For instance, women caregivers, compared with women who are not caregivers, are less likely to:

- Get needed medical care
- Fill a prescription because of the cost
- Get a mammogram

Also, caregivers report that, compared with the time before they became caregivers, they are less likely to:

- Get enough sleep
- Cook healthy meals
- Get enough physical activity

How can I tell if caregiving is putting too much stress on me?

> ### Helpful Hint
>
> *Lori advises: To begin with, never dismiss your feelings as "just stress."*
> *Caregiver stress can lead to serious health problems and you should take steps to reduce it as much as you can.*

Caregiving may be putting too much stress on you if you have any of the following symptoms:

- Feeling overwhelmed
- Sleeping too much or too little
- Gaining or losing a lot of weight
- Feeling tired most of the time
- Loss of interest in activities you used to enjoy
- Becoming easily irritated or angered
- Feeling constantly worried
- Often feeling sad
- Frequent headaches, bodily pain, or other physical problems
- Abuse of alcohol or drugs, including prescription drugs

What can I do to prevent or relieve stress?

Research shows that people who take an active, problem-solving approach to caregiving issues are less likely to feel stressed than those who react by worrying or feeling helpless. Some hospitals offer classes that can teach you how to care for someone with the disease that your loved one is facing. To find these classes, ask your doctor, contact an organization that focuses on this disease, or call your local Area Agency on Aging. Other good sources of caregiving information include:

- Doctors and nurses
- Library books
- Websites of disease-specific organizations

Here are some more tips for reducing stress:

- Find out about caregiving resources in your community (see below).
- Ask for and accept help. Be prepared with a mental list of ways that others can help you, and let the helper choose what she would like to do. For instance, one person might be happy to take the person you care for on a walk a couple times a week. Someone else might be glad to pick up some groceries for you.

- If you need financial help taking care of a relative, don't be afraid to ask family members to contribute their fair share.
- Say "no" to requests that are draining, such as hosting holiday meals.
- Don't feel guilty that you are not a "perfect" caregiver. Just as there is no "perfect parent," there is no such thing as a "perfect caregiver." You're doing the best you can.
- Identify what you can and cannot change. You may not be able to change someone else's behavior, but you can change the way that you react to it.
- Set realistic goals. Break large tasks into smaller steps that you can do one at a time.
- Prioritize, make lists, and establish a daily routine.
- Stay in touch with family and friends.
- Join a support group for caregivers in your situation, such as caring for someone with dementia. Besides being a great way to make new friends, you can also pick up some caregiving tips from others who are facing the same problems you are.
- Make time each week to do something that you want to do, such as go to a movie.
- Try to find time to be physically active on most days of the week, eat a healthy diet, and get enough sleep.
- See your doctor for a checkup. Tell her that you are a caregiver and tell her about any symptoms of depression or sickness you may be having.
- Try to keep your sense of humor.

If you work outside the home and are feeling overwhelmed, consider taking a break from your job. Employees covered under the federal Family and Medical Leave Act may be able to take up to 12 weeks of unpaid leave per year to care for relatives. Ask your human resources office about options for unpaid leave.

There are also devices that you can buy that can help you make sure that your loved one is safe. Here are some examples:

- Emergency response systems involve a button on a necklace, bracelet, or belt that your loved one wears. If she has an emergency and you are not home, she presses the button to alert a monitoring center. The center then alerts medical personnel and you. These systems are intended for people who can press the button and do not have dementia.

- An intercom system allows you to hear your loved one from another area of your home.
- A Webcam is a video camera that allows you to see your loved one from another area of your home.
- Mobility monitors use a small transmitter to help keep track of people with dementia. When your loved one wearing a transmitter strapped to her ankle or wrist passes out of a set range, the transmitter alerts you that your loved one is wandering away.

Also, researchers are developing technologies to allow doctors and nurses to examine and treat patients from locations different than the patient's. This new field is called telemedicine. It uses a communication system, like the Internet or two-way television, to collect medical information and provide instructions to the caregiver and patient. Telemedicine will be most useful in rural areas where few doctors are available. Some states already have limited telemedicine programs in operation.

Besides Medicare and Medicaid, there is another federal program, called the National Family Caregiver Support Program, that helps states provide services for family caregivers. To be eligible for the program, a caregiver must:

- Care for an adult aged 60 years and older, or
- Care for a person of any age with Alzheimer's disease or a related disorder

More information on caregiver stress

For more information about caregiver stress, call womenshealth.gov at 800-994-9662 (TDD: 888-220-5446) or contact the following organizations:

- **Centers for Medicare and Medicaid Services**
  - ° **www.cms.hhs.gov**
  - ° **Phone:** 800-633-4227

- **Eldercare Locator, Administration on Aging, HHS**
  - ○ www.eldercare.gov
  - ○ **Phone: 800-677-1116**
- **Family Caregiver Alliance**
  - ○ www.caregiver.org
  - ○ **Phone: 800-445-8106**
- **National Alliance for Caregiving**
  - ○ **www.caregiving.gov**
- **National Family Caregivers Association**
  - ○ www.nfacares.org
  - ○ **Phone: 800-896-3650**
- **The National Respite Locator Service**
  - ○ www.respitelocater.org
  - ○ **Phone: 919-490-5577**

*Source: Office on Women's Health in the Office of the Assistant Secretary for Health at the U.S. Department of Health and Human Services .

Chapter Twelve

The Final Move

Six months after Mom's move, I had had it. I felt like I did not have a weekend to call my own. So, Dick and I decided to accept an invitation to spend Thanksgiving with friends at their mountain get-a-way. We told everyone that we would not be back until Sunday night, but slipped back into town on Saturday evening. When I listened to the messages on our telephone answering machine, I heard my sister-in-law's voice telling me that Mom had been rushed to the hospital. My brother had had dinner with her and was fortunately with her when she apparently had a heart attack. They needed her medical insurance and Medicare information as well as info on her new doctors, all information that I knew how to locate. After a brief visit to her apartment to collect the necessary documents, I was at the hospital in record time. Times have certainly changed thanks to modern technology. Today, I email that information to myself and save it at an online site so it is accessible wherever I may be and that antiquated answering machine has been replaced by the ubiquitous cell phone so you are always available, for better or worse, 24/7 365 days of the year.

I got there as the doctor came out of the emergency room to inquire whether or not heroic measures were to be taken as Mom, they then thought, had had a massive heart attack. As it turned out, her heart attack was minor, the scarring on the muscle having been caused by her prior heart attacks. In fact, what she really had was pneumonia which had precipitated a small heart attack. Her regular doctor was located, his partner, on call for the holiday weekend, took over management of her case.

This little story had a happy ending. But what if she had been far from home? If we hadn't been there to say "Yes, take aggressive measures to save her life." would doctors have treated what they saw not as our Mom, but just another old woman, the way she deserved to be treated?

I felt guilty that the first weekend in six months I had not spent with Mom was the one on which she became critically ill. But things got better.

Mom enjoyed three more happy years filled with grandchildren's birthday parties, coffee dates with Dick, outings around D.C. including a much anticipated visit to the Holocaust Museum. When she did become critically ill, we were with her and able to provide support and love.

What did we learn from all of this that is changing our own behavior as we get older? Well, the house on three levels with too many stairs and too much physical upkeep is gone. Instead we live in a "white glove" coop in Manhattan where our every need can be taken care of. We order dinner from Fresh Direct (a great fresh food delivery company), the dry cleaner is in the building, public transportation is, for the most part, "friendly" to the aging and the handicapped and conveniently located right on the corner where we live. We sold our car when we moved to the city and now take the bus, cabs and the occasional "black car" service. There is no stigma to not driving in Manhattan and unlike Mom, I am not reluctant to take a cab when the weather is bad or I am in a hurry to get somewhere.

Selling Estate Property

We bought our coop as an estate sale and realize that at some point in the future we will have to decide whether staying here "forever" makes sense and if it does, what are the implications for our own heirs. Coops are tricky and at some point we will take our own advice and speak to an attorney who is expert in this area of the world and of the law.

According to Matt Abrams, the same factors that are viewed as the benefits of co-op ownership – exclusivity and high standards for the tenants in a co-op – can pose problems when it comes to sell the apartment. Boards can and do turn away candidates they deem "unsuitable," often for reasons that are less than clear. While Federal and state law prevents co-op boards from legally discriminating against prospective purchasers due to race, color, national origin, religion, sex, family status, or disability, finances may be subject to scrutiny, references may be examined in detail, and the purchaser must generally make a good impression on board members. In a practical sense, a board's managing agents can also cause delays in the course of due diligence before the contract of sale is signed and in the board review and approval process.

If the board declines to grant approval to the purchase, the sale is over: if the denial is due to the purchaser's bad faith – examples include refusing to comply with the Board's reasonable requests or refusing to meet with the Board – then the seller may be able to keep the contract deposit. If not, the seller may have to refund the deposit and start the listing, negotiating, and approval process all over again. One way to address the issue of financial suitability of a purchaser is to request representations in the contract or rider regarding the same items into which the co-op board will inquire – bankruptcies, previous rejections by other co-op or condo boards, credit account defaults, tax liens, and the like. If the purchaser makes these representations falsely, the seller has a stronger case for keeping the contract deposit.

If your parent has occupied the apartment for several years, he or she may not know the location of the original stock certificate and proprietary lease. Both documents will be required for closing, and if you do not have/cannot find them, the managing agent and/or co-op will almost certainly charge a fee for replacing them. Keep in mind that if the apartment is subject to an existing mortgage, the lender may be holding these documents in their files, and you will need to request that they be produced along with the "payoff statement" for the mortgage balance.

Other fees associated with the sale are generally limited, but the Board may have instituted a "Flip Tax" – either a percentage of sale price or a dollar amount per share – of which your parent may be generally

Helpful Hints

The census bureau reports that 31% of home owners over 65 do indeed have a mortgage.

If you find yourself inheriting a mortgage as well as property, check immediately with the attorney for the estate as to the conditions included in the mortgage document and the availability of liquid funds to pay this and other expenses.

unaware. The existence of this fee may not make the listing and sale more difficult, but it is another factor to be taken into account when calculating your parent's financial needs in connection the sale price.

Beyond these issues, the same one's discussed in Chapter Five will apply – authority, money, and practical issues of moving and the closing. The most common encumbrance on title is an existing security interest – the co-op equivalent of a mortgage. Judgments and liens may also have to be resolved before closing or will be satisfied by a portion (or all) of the purchase price, depending on the nature of the obligation.

After The Funeral

When Mom died, I sold her apartment. Fortunately, it was a condo, not a coop and there was no mortgage. As it had been brand new when she bought it, not much needed to be done. I did, however, have the apartment professionally cleaned, painted and re-carpeted. It was worth every penny and we got a full price offer within 10 days. There was no mortgage on the property so the carrying costs were low – limited to the maintenance and monthly tax charges, but we did not want to deplete my mother's small estate with payments for an apartment that no one was using. As the executor of her estate, I could use funds from the estate to pay the carrying costs and make the improvements necessary for a prompt sale. If there is a mortgage, you should make certain that the executor keeps the payments current to avoid penalties or liens against the property. Fortunately, there were just two beneficiaries to the estate, just my brother and myself and he basically deferred to me to "get it done". According to Matt Abrams, if there are several beneficiaries, it is important to keep everyone informed about what is needed to get done so that there are no complaints afterwards.

The census bureau reports that 31% of home owners over 65 do indeed have a mortgage. If you find yourself inheriting a mortgage as well as property, check immediately with the attorney for the estate as to the conditions included in the mortgage document and the availability of liquid funds to pay this and other expenses.

We also used a real estate agent who specialized in the building and in dealing with elder care issues. If your apartment or your loved one's is in "estate" condition you will probably have to do more than just tidy up. Despite Matt's advice to list in "as is" condition, I am sure Barbara would agree that a fresh coat of paint and good looking floors, be they carpet or hardwood, go a long way toward making the apartment appeal to a potential buyer. A stager can help you decide how much needs to be done and how to work with what you have. Clutter, dingy paint and dated furnishings will bring down the price.

Barbara Brock reminds us that there is more to do after the funeral than stage the apartment and list it for sale.

Barbara says: Having been called in to handle the staging of many estates in New York City, part of the process has been to help the heir(s) or attorney in dispersing the household and personal possessions ("items"). These have been my observations when there is no clear designation in advance:

- There is a stronger emotional connection to a parent than to a sibling and this may cause delay in wanting to disperse "items".
- There is confusion about what to do with all the "items" (sell, keep, donate, toss).
- There is confusion about how to value the "items" (by appraisal evaluation of every object, by every heir stating what they want, by a designated person)
- There may be different opinions on how to disperse "items" (call in outside services, do it yourself)
- The amount of time it takes to sort out the household can be especially hard on an out of town heir.
- The time period may be different for one person than another to receive "Items", thereby delaying the process.
- Tensions mount when someone doesn't think they are getting a "fair" share.
- The longer the delay to make decisions and disperse "items" decreases the amount to the heir.

For all of these reasons,
- I suggest beginning the conversation with your parent, find out if they have a preference for the jewelry, art, furniture, etc.
- You may be surprised - they will have thought about who they'd like to receive what.

- Talking with your siblings and heirs ahead of time can avoid a lot of bad feelings, especially if the heir is turning over the decision to his or her spouse.

Barbara adds: Recently my mother passed away. There are 7 children in the family and we were the only heirs to the estate. Beforehand. Mother had designated the distribution of her jewelry and we children had discussed important pieces that we'd like to have. (Remember our earlier tip to photograph all of the items before the move – this works even if there is not a move involved.) After the funeral, we gathered to hear the will and talk about mom's furniture, accessories and art. It was first decided that if one of our spouses wanted anything, they had to tell the heir and it had to be part of that heir's request. Seven people were enough to make decisions!

I had brought the list of designated items, my sister brought the estate appraisal and one of my brothers brought 7 packets of different colors of sticky notes. We could have valued every piece in the estate, divided up a monetary equal portion for everyone and spent time in calculating and hassling over a "fair" share. Instead, we opted for the sticky note method. If a piece of furniture, art or accessory had many colored sticky notes, then those people had to make the decision. This was a huge success. There were far less items which had multiple sticky notes than you might think.

Buying from an Estate

As I mentioned, Dick and I purchased from an estate and knew that we would be doing a gut renovation. Nonetheless, the agent representing the heirs had hired a stager who got rid of some of the tattered furnishings replacing them with comfortable seating that encouraged those looking at the apartment to sit and enjoy the fabulous light. You can change the paint, you can't fix the light! The stager helped the agent to emphasize the apartment's strength and it worked. When we walked in, my first thought was "what a dump!" Dick's was "What great light!"

Buying from an estate complicated the purchase process to a certain degree. The coop board required that all executors be present at the closing rather than enabling them to provide a power of attorney. As this estate had two surviving heirs who lived in different states, coordinating their schedules with those of the attorneys for each side and the managing agent was a bit tricky. If you are purchasing from an estate, make certain that the real estate agents for both sides of the transaction are aware of your needs. While you cannot necessarily control the amount of time a board takes to review your application and schedule a board interview, you can put a prospective move-in date into your contract of sale.

You should also be cognizant of whether or not the apartment has been vacant for a period of time. In our case, we found that the "air-handlers" were caked with dust and not functioning properly because the apartment had been vacant for nearly two years and the equipment had not been serviced during that period of time. Fortunately, it was easy to rectify this problem, but it took a couple of months to discover that we had a problem. When we signed our contract for the purchase, we knew we would be doing a gut renovation so we did not bother to specify the working condition of the appliances. However, as is standard practice in New York and typical in other areas as well, we needed to get board approval for the renovation. We were actually fortunate that it only took three months to hire an architect have the drawings produced and have the building's architect approve our plan. To save money, we decided to live in the apartment until we began the renovation. Before we moved from our rental to our "new" coop, we conferred with our mover and put the majority of our possessions and clothing into storage, moving only the bare necessities, one couch and our bed.

Late on the first evening in our new place, we had a food delivery. To our horror and surprise the refrigerator did not work properly! Fortunately, our building engineer was able to switch it out for another old, but functioning refrigerator that had been discarded during another owner's renovation.

A year and six months of architect drawings, marathon purchases and great contractors later, we are enjoying our totally renovated apartment. It is just enough space for us, not too big and no stairs!

Appendix

Author Bio

Susan Phillips Bari brings to her new career as a licensed real estate salesperson the marketing and customer service experience gained in a diverse career at the top of organizations in the public, nonprofit and entrepreneurial sectors. As a former Associate Director of Presidential Personnel in The White House, Bari learned to perfectly match job candidates with their dream jobs. As founding President of the Women's Business Enterprise National Council, Susan found satisfaction in matching woman-owned business suppliers with corporate buyers. Today, what was once an avocation, a passion for property, is now a career in real estate sales. Bari works with buyers to find each the perfect home and with sellers to create marketing strategies that bring buyers to their doorstep.

Bari received her MBA from Virginia Tech where she serves on the Business Advisory Council to the Pamplin College of Business and her BA with a major in English Literature from the University of Massachusetts. A firm believer in life-long learning, Bari also has certificates from the John F. Kennedy School of Government, Harvard College, Program for Senior Managers in Government and Milano, The New School, Tenenbaum Leadership Initiative and recently earned the national designation as a Certified Negotiation Expert (CNE) from the Real Estate Negotiation Institute. Bari is the author of Breaking Through: Creating Opportunities for America's Women and Minority Owned Businesses, Partnering for Profit: Success Strategies for Tomorrow's Supply Chain, and Yes! I Can Do That. She writes a monthly e-newsletter *"Susan Sells New York."*

Contributor Biographies

Matthew B. Abrams is an associate in the firm of Russo & Burke in New York City. He is admitted to practice in the State of New York and in the U.S. District Courts for the Southern and Eastern Districts of New York. Mr. Abrams' practice focuses on the areas of trusts and estates, real estate and labor and employment. He is a member of the American Bar Association and the New York State Bar Association. He earned his B.A. from Columbia University in 2004 and his J.D. from New York Law School in 2007. Mr. Abrams advises and has represented clients in litigation and administration of estates and trusts in the five boroughs of New York City and Suffolk, Nassau, Orange and Westchester Counties. He regularly counsels elderly and estate clients on matters of real estate purchases, sales and rentals.

The firm of **Russo & Burke** was founded in 1984 by William J. Russo and Joseph M. Burke. The firm is located at 600 Third Avenue in Manhattan's Murray Hill neighborhood and operates within the Russo & Burke Law Suite, which provides solo practitioners and small firms with a congenial professional atmosphere and the ability to confer with experts in and beyond their practices. Our website can be accessed at **http://www.russoandburke.com**, and consultations can be arranged by contacting our office manager at (888) 381-7085.

Barbara Brock, founder of **A Proper Place** which launched in 2001, initially focused on professional organizing, but quickly evolved the focus of the firm into Home Staging in 2003. Her company quickly grew through word of mouth referrals from and impressive media coverage. In 2012, she and Jay Hart, formed **SOLD WITH STYLE** to expand her offerings to include a 5,000 square foot warehouse of furniture and the input of Manhattan's top staging designers.

A native Texan, Brock earned a Bachelor of Science in Mathematics from Southern Methodist University, and later, a Design Certificate from Parson's School of Design in New York. In Manhattan, she worked for celebrated interior designers Harry Schnaper and Mark Hampton and credits her roles with them as the foundation upon which her skills as a design entrepreneur are built: project organization, design history and theory, effective solutions in time-sensitive circumstances.

In 2008, Brock started the New York Chapter of RESA (Real Estate Staging Association) and served as its President for two years. She's currently Program Director of RESA-NY , and is a continuing member of NAPO, National Association of Professional Organizers.

Her work has been featured on the Martha Stewart Morning Show and Sirius Radio as well as in The New York Times and the Long Island Gazette.

Cynthia Myer is the President/CEO of Ridgewood Moving Services, Co., Bergen County, New Jersey's premiere Moving and Storage Company.

Under Ms. Myers leadership, Ridgewood Moving is a certified woman owned business, agent for Arpin Van lines and holds the elite status of Circle of Excellence in the state. She continues to raise the bar in a mostly male-dominated industry, encouraging training, consumer awareness and becoming a resource and leader in relocations.   In addition to the many services Ridgewood Moving provides, Ms. Myer has dedicated a Senior Move niche in the industry and division within her company.

Ms. Myer is a member of many industry groups serves on the Executive Board of the New Jersey Warehousemen and Movers Association.

Cynthia Myer is actively engaged in the community, donating her trucks, material and labor throughout the year and serves on the board of Shelter Our Sisters, a not for profit agency providing shelter and safety for victims of domestic violence.

Lori Sokol, Ph.D., is President of Sokol Media, Inc., publisher of Work Life Matters magazine, Green Matters magazine, and NY Residential magazine. Dr. Sokol effectively combines her experience as the publisher of real estate development industry magazines with her training and credentials in the field of Psychology to provide insight and analysis about the spaces in which we choose to live and work. Her articles on this subject have been published in the Huffington Post, Slate.com and the Baltimore Sun, and she is the author of The Agile Workplace & Workforce: The New Future of Work (Bonnier, 2011).

Made in the USA
Charleston, SC
25 April 2012